Also by Lisa Lillien

Hungry Girl:
Recipes and Survival Strategies
for Guilt-Free Eating in the Real World

Hungry Girl 200 Under 200:
200 Recipes Under 200 Calories

Hungry Girl: The Official Survival Guides:
Tips & Tricks for Guilt-Free Eating
(audio book)

Hungry Girl Chew the Right Thing:
Supreme Makeovers for 50 Foods You Crave
(recipe cards)

Hungry Girl

1-2-3

The Easiest, Most Delicious, Guilt-Free Recipes on the Planet

Lisa Lillien

St. Martin's Griffin

New York

HUNGRY GIRL 1-2-3: THE EASIEST, MOST DELICIOUS, GUILT-FREE RECIPES ON THE PLANET. Copyright © 2010 by Hungry Girl, Inc. All rights reserved. Printed in the United States of America. For information, address St. Martin's Press, 175 Fifth Avenue, New York, N.Y. 10010.

www.stmartins.com

Cover design and book design by Elizabeth Hodson

Illustrations by Jack Pullan

Food styling and photography by General Mills Photography Studios

      Photographer: Andy Swarbrick

      Food Stylists: Amy Peterson and Carol Grones

      Art Director: Chris Everett

ISBN 978-0-312-55618-1

First Edition: April 2010

10 9 8 7 6 5 4 3 2 1

The book is dedicated to
the memory of Cookie, the
sweetest, kissiest, hungriest, most
inspirational and special little
friend anyone ever had.

Contents

Acknowledgments   xiii

Introduction   2
The 411 on *HG 1-2-3*
Kitchen Staples and Recommended Products

Chapter 1   ## Swingin' Single Meals   8
Pizza Luau
AM Apple Scramble
Tremendous Top-Shelf Turkey Burger
Outside-In Cheeseburger Patty
Cheesy Green Eggs 'n Hamwiches
Smothered Pepperoni Pizza Breakfast Burrito
Totally Thai Chicken Lettuce Cups
Lucky Four-Leaf Salad with Feta and Apples
Honey Mustard Pretzel-Coated Chicken Fingers
Santa Fe Cheesy Chicken Stir-Fry
Totally Terrific Tuna Melt
Pizza-fied Chicken
Chop-Chop Beef Stir-Fry
Too-Beautiful Turkey Burger
Bowling for Pizza
Sausage, Peppers, and Onions Italia

Chapter 2   ## Fast & for Two (or Three, or Four!)   40
Three-Cheese Bacon-Apple-Bella Frittata
Shrimp & Grits . . . for Hungry Chicks!
Amazin' Asian Ahi Tuna Burgers
Good Chick Lollipops
Spring Chicken Skillet
Fiesta Noodle Casserole
Chicken D'lish Kebabs
Planet Hungrywood Sweet & Cap'n Crunchy Chicken
Aloha Under the Sea
Girl-on-Grill Veggie Wraps
Pan-Fried Chicken Parm
Veggie-rific Fried Rice
Te Quiero Tequila Shrimp
Devil-icious Shrimp
Chicken Enchilada Casserole

Chapter 3   Nuke It, Baby!   68

College Breakfast Burrito
Egg Mug Florentine
Egg Mug Burger-rama
Egg McMuggin'
Egg Mug Lorraine
Egg Mug Mexicali
Sausage Spaghetti Swap
Cheesy Beefy Supreme Wrap
Italian-Style Bacon Alfredo Bowl
BLT Pasta Salad
Buffalo Vegetable Hungry Girlfredo
Sloppy Joe-chiladas
Buff Chick Hot Wing Dip
Cup o' Chocolate-Coconut Bread Pudding
Cake on the Beach
Expresso Cake in a Mug

Chapter 4   Four Ingredients or Less   90

The American Classic Pita
Grillin' of the Corn
Stuffed Chick Cordon Bleu
Backyard BBQ Beef Cups
Too-EZ Mac 'n Cheese
Shrimp Cocktail Tacos
Cheesy Crab 'n Chile Quesadilla
Creamed Corn-Cheese Bites
Quickie Caramel Custard
BFFs (Black Forest Fillo-Cups)

Chapter 5   Cook-Me-Not   106

Ginormous Sweet-Tart Fruit Salad
Salmon Spread the Love
Crab-Happy Sunomono Salad
Twice-Tomatoed Turkey Tortilla
Slammin' Slaw
Shrimped-Up Sweet Corn 'n Tomato Salad
Gazpacho Surprise
Veggie-Packed Wrap Attack
Double-O-Cinnamon Apple Breakfast Bowl

Chapter 6   Fast Food Faves . . . Fast!   120

Big Bowl of Breakfast
No-Buns-About-It Animal-Style Cheeseburger
Sweet 'n Sassy Boneless Hot Wings
Chili-rific Cheeseburger
Island Insanity Burger
Blue-Ribbon Roast Beef Sandwich
Queen-of-the-Castle Sliders
Bursting Burrito Bowl
Chili Cheese Dog Nachos

Chapter 7   Foiled Again . . . and Again . . . and Again   140

Glaze-of-Sunshine Apricot Chicken
So-Fancy Fish Pack
Mom-Style Creamy Chicken 'n Veggies
Chicken-with-a-Kick Pack
Caribbean Shrimp Packets
The Rat(atouille) Pack
Crazy Pineapple Salmon Teriyaki
Happy Camper Cheeseburger Crumble
Stuffed 'n Squashed Mushroom Foil Pack
Hustle 'n Brussels Foil-Pack Attack
Fajitas in a Foil Pack
Do the Cabbage Pack!
Easy Oven-Baked S'mores-Stuffed Bananas
Fruity Fish Fillet Foil Packs
HG's Oven-to-Grill Foil-Pack Conversion Chart

Chapter 8   Crock Around the Clock   170

Crazy-Delicious Seafood Corn Chowder
Slow-Cookin' BBQ Chicken
Chunky Veggie Pumpkin Chili
Pump-Up-the-Jam Cocktail Weenies
Dan-Good Cioppino
Turkey Mushroom Surprise
Slow-Cookin' Mexican Chicken
Glaze-of-Glory Candied Carrots
EZ as 1-2-3-Alarm Turkey Chili
Sweet-Hot Steak Bites
Hungry Chick Chunky Soup

Chapter 9   Things That Go Blend   192

Slush-Puppy Pineapple Lemonade
Pretty-in-Pink Slushie Drink
Cherry Lemonade Super-Slushie
Cool 'n Creamy Fruit Soup
Creamy Dreamy Portabella Soup
Peachy-Keen Black Bean Soup
Creamy Caramelized Onion Bisque
Chilla in Vanilla Milkshake
Chocolate-Covered-Cherries Freeze
Slurpable Split Shake
Pumpkin-licious Nog
Toffee Crush Coffee Shake
Make-Mine-Mint Cookie-rific Ice Cream Freeze
Pumpkin Pie Smoothie
Mud Pie in the Sky

Chapter 10   Speedy Sweeties   216

Apple Shakers
Dessert Island Parfait
Super-Simple Apple-Cinnamon Dessert Crepes
Big Black-and-White Berry Parfait
Gimme S'more Sundae
Caramel Swirl Cream Puffs
Oatmeal Raisin Softies
Peanut Butter Oatmeal Softies
Upside-Down Personal Key Lime Pies
Hot Fudge 'n Brownie Blitz
Upside-Down Pineapple Crush
That's Hazel-NUTS! Cocoa Supreme
Scoopable Creamsicle Crush Pie

Chapter 11   EZ & Crowd-Pleasy   238

Oven-Baked Omelette Lasagna
Perfect Pumpkin Bread
Fruity Bruschetta
Exploding Chicken Taquitos
Tomato Bacon Tarts
Corndog Millionaire Muffins
Fiesta Bites
Yumbo Gumbo
Sloppy Franks

Holy Moly Cannoli Cones
Jammin' Tarts
Frosted Apple Pie Cupcakes

Chapter 12   Fun with . . . Broccoli Cole Slaw   264

Sweet 'n Chunky Turkey Slaw
Bacon Ranch Broccoli Slaw
Teriyaki Shrimp 'n Slaw Stir-Fry
BBQ Chicken Slaw
Saucy Pasta Swap
Mmmmm Moo Shu Chicken
Turkey & Veggie Meatloaf Minis
Greek Chicken Salad Slaw
Hawaiian Slaw

Chapter 12½   Fun with . . . French Toast   278

French-Toasted Waffles
Cinnamon French Toast Bowl-a-rama
The Big Apple French Toast Casserole
Super-Cheesy Ham-Stuffed French Toast
Cannoli-Stuffed French Toast Nuggets
Overstuffed Peanut Butter 'n Banana French Toast
Pumpkin Cheesecake French Toast Bites
Jammed with Cheese Stuffed French Toast

Bonus Section   Hot Couples!   294

Starring . . . Yogurt
Starring . . . Rice Cakes
Starring . . . Pudding Snacks
Starring . . . Laughing Cow Light
Starring . . . Frozen Fruit
Starring . . . Frozen Broccoli & Cheese Sauce
Starring . . . Broccoli Cole Slaw
Fast Food Combos
Dessert Duos
Protein-Packed Pairs
Breakfast Twosomes

Afterword   319

Index   321

Acknowledgments

Even though this book is filled with SIMPLE recipes, it was anything but easy to put together. The following people deserve credit, along with me, for helping put it together and for helping to make Hungry Girl so successful:

To the HG Editorial & Production Staff...

Jamie Goldberg—You bleed PINK. Your endless hard work and dedication to Hungry Girl are appreciated more than any existing words can express. I'm toying with the idea of making some up (or just choreographing an expressive interpretive dance). Thank you times infinity.

Alison Kreuch—Thank you for being you. You're a bundle of energy and pretty much the Tasmanian Devil of the marketing & advertising world. (And I truly mean that in the best way possible.)

Lynn Bettencourt—You've been a tremendous asset to HG for more than three years now. Hope there are many more to come. Oh, and . . . CHICKEN!!!

Lisa Friedman—Friedman, you're solid. And super-reliable. Thank you for ALWAYS being levelheaded, organized, and super-duper-nice.

Dana DeRuyck—You are AWESOME and talented and incredibly valued. Your energy always brightens up the HG HQ. You rule!

Callie Pegadiotes—We're glad you found us in San Diego. LOVE having you as part of the team. Thank you for everything you do.

Jennifer Curtis—You STILL live too far away. Would you move already so you can work with us full-time? Pretty please . . . with Fat Free Reddi-wip on top?!

Lisa Foiles—You're a Photoshop whiz. Thanks for making our emails beauteous and for the super-fast, fantastic work. Wish you were here with us in L.A.

Adam Feinsilver—You're a video guru. Plain and simple. Thanks for bringing HG to life on the monitor. And for the silly fun at the office.

Special thanks to **Elizabeth Hodson**—It was extremely sad to lose you (the FIRST HG employee) as an official HG staffer in 2009. We miss you. You know you ALWAYS have an open invite to come back. Thank you for staying on as the official HG book designer and for helping to make this book our most adorable, gorgeous, and DELICIOUS one yet.

More Thank-Yous...

John Vaccaro—You continue to be an invaluable asset to Hungry Girl, but more importantly, you're also an irreplaceable friend.

Neeti Madan—I used to say you're the best agent on the planet, but at this point I am pretty sure you rule the entire galaxy. Thank you.

Matthew Shear and **Jennifer Enderlin**—I am the luckiest author to have you both. I sincerely hope we work together forever...

John Karle—You're an awesome publicist. We're in year three and going strong! Lots more fun to come... Thank you, thank you!

Anne Marie Tallberg—You're amazing and so much fun to work with. And you never get frazzled. (How is that possible?)

John Murphy—We don't work together as much as I'd like, but I love you anyway. (Air kisses... both sides!)

Advisors and Friends...

Tom Fineman—You're the world's most effective and likable attorney. Hands down.

Jeff Becker—I know you hate guilt-free food. But I still enjoy you. Thanks for all the advice and guidance.

Bill Stankey—Thank you for appreciating the things about me that should make you want to strangle me. Truly.

But Wait, There's More...

Huge thanks to **Jack Pullan, David Witt,** and to **Nanci Dixon** and the amazing General Mills photography crew. Without you guys, the book wouldn't have pretty pictures and fantastic illustrations. And to **Val Pensky,** for all the tour support and for being the best travel companion. To **Gary Stromberg**, for all of the INSANELY awesome stuff. To **Eileen Opatut**, for being super-smart and fun to work with. And to **Pete Austria**, for making me lift heavy objects from time to time.

The BIG Finish...

Thanks also to my amazing mom and dad, **Florence** and **Maurice Lillien,** for making me super-hungry. And to **Meri Lillien, Jay Lillien,** and to the **Lillien** and **Schneider families**—Love you all.

To **Jackson**—Thank you for keeping me warm while I email at 6am. You're a lovely beast. To my close personal pals, the Hungry Girl subscribers—YOU TRULY ROCK. All 1,000,000 of you. Thank you!!!!!

And to my husband, **Daniel Schneider**—Thank you for always being there and for always being right. About pretty much everything. And also for continuing to make me laugh louder and harder every year. I LOVE YOU.

The 411 on *HG 1-2-3*...

Welcome to *Hungry Girl 1-2-3: The Easiest, Most Delicious, Guilt-Free Recipes on the Planet*. This is the THIRD HG cookbook and I LOVE it. I'm pretty sure you will, too. Why? Well, like our other books, it's PACKED with great recipes for fantastic-tasting foods that are low in calories and fat grams. But this book is different, in some ways, and quite possibly the best of the bunch. (I hope we always keep getting better and better!) Here are the key things that make this book super-amazing and SO EASY to use . . . and, um, some other relevant stuff as well!

1. There are more fresh fruits, veggies, and lean protein in the recipes than ever before.

We listened, and they're all here.

2. Fast and easy recipes.

The name says it all. It's not like Hungry Girl recipes are ever THAT complicated—you know this. But the recipes in this book are crazy-simple to make. Like, easier than any other recipes anywhere. Really. There are entire chapters devoted to microwavable recipes, recipes with four ingredients or less, and recipes that require no cooking whatsoever!

3. So many meals!!!

In *200 Under 200*, we loaded you up on snacks. This time around, there's more of a focus on entrées. DELICIOUS ones.

4. New recipe format.

We decided it was time to make the leap. Now the ingredients are listed in the order they're used, and each recipe starts off by listing some kitchen essentials along with the approximate prep and cook times. There are also lots of useful tips, plus notes on recipes that call for a common ingredient or two, so opened products don't have to go to waste. Soooooo helpful!

5. Your crock-pot prayers have been answered.

You asked for more, and now you've got 'em. There's an entire chapter devoted to crock-pot recipes. Party time!

6. Foil-pack recipes GALORE.

Wrapping stuff in foil and baking it couldn't be easier. Our foil-pack recipes have become so popular, I thought it would be great to include a full chapter of them . . . so I did. There are even easy-to-follow instructions for adapting these recipes to be made on the grill. Yay!

7. Couples.

Our two-ingredient recipes have become so beloved, I wanted to carve out an entire section of the book for them. And that's what I did. There are more than 60 food duos here!

8. Photos and *POINTS*®.

As always, photos for every single recipe in this book along with Weight Watchers *POINTS*® values* can be found at hungry-girl.com/book.

Happy chewing!!!!

Lisa :)

The Points® values for these recipes were calculated by Hungry Girl and are not an endorsement or approval of the recipe or its developer by Weight Watchers International, Inc., the owner of the Points® registered trademark.

Kitchen Staples and Recommended Products

We're keeping things simple. Here are some frequently used HG basics to have on hand, plus some specific products we LOVE . . .

Pantry

Splenda No Calorie Sweetener (granulated)
No-calorie sweetener packets
> *Splenda*

Whole-wheat flour
Old-fashioned oats
Nonstick cooking spray
Low-fat honey graham crackers
Rice cakes
Mini semi-sweet chocolate chips
25-calorie packets diet hot cocoa mix
> *Swiss Miss Diet*

Canned black beans
Canned crushed tomatoes
Canned diced tomatoes
Canned pineapple packed in juice (crushed, rings, and tidbits)
Canned pure pumpkin
> *Libby's*

Fridge

Fat-free liquid egg substitute
> *Egg Beaters Original*

Light whipped butter or light buttery spread
Brummel & Brown, Land O' Lakes Whipped Light Butter
Light vanilla soymilk (or another light vanilla milk product)
8th Continent Light
Blue Diamond Unsweetened Vanilla Almond Breeze
The Laughing Cow Light Original Swiss cheese wedges
Light string cheese
Jell-O Sugar Free Pudding Snacks
Fat-free yogurt
Yoplait Light, Fiber One, Fage Total 0% Greek yogurt
Reduced-fat Parmesan-style grated topping
Reduced-sodium/lite soy sauce
Sugar-free pancake syrup
Log Cabin Sugar Free, Mrs. Butterworth's Sugar Free
Hellmann's/Best Foods Dijonnaise
Fat-free or nearly fat-free franks
Hebrew National 97% Fat Free Beef Franks
Hoffy Extra Lean Beef Franks
Precooked real crumbled bacon
Oscar Mayer, Hormel
Turkey bacon or center-cut bacon
Pillsbury Crescent Recipe Creations Seamless Dough Sheet
House Foods Tofu Shirataki Noodle Substitute (stocked with the tofu)
Broccoli cole slaw
Mann's Sunny Shores

Fresh Produce

Romaine lettuce
Onions
Bell peppers
Cucumbers
Tomatoes
Fuji apples

Freezer

Boneless skinless lean chicken breast cutlets
Shrimp
Fish fillets
Boca Original Meatless Burger (Vegan)
Ground-beef-style soy crumbles
      Boca Meatless Ground Crumbles
      Morningstar Farms Meal Starters Grillers Recipe Crumbles
Green Giant Just for One Broccoli & Cheese Sauce
Assorted vegetables
Unsweetened fruit
Cool Whip Free

Breadbox

Does anyone HAVE an actual breadbox anymore?

Light bread (40 to 45 calories and at least 2 grams of fiber per slice)
> *Sara Lee Delightful, Nature's Own Light*

Light English muffins (high in fiber with about 100 calories each)

Burrito-size tortillas with about 110 calories (high in fiber, low in fat)
> *La Tortilla Factory Smart & Delicious*
> *Low Carb High Fiber*
> *Mission Carb Balance*
> *Tumaro's 8" Low in Carbs*
> *or Healthy Flour Tortillas*
> *Flatout Light Wraps*

chapter one | Swingin' Single Meals

Meals for one are super-popular in HG-land!

The best thing about these recipes is that even though they were designed as single-serves, it's easy to turn them into multi-serving recipes for a group. Just double, triple, or quadruple the ingredient amounts accordingly. Sometimes, you won't even need a calculator. Yes, it really is that simple.

pizza luau

This pizza is sweet, fun, and DELICIOUS. And don't even *think* about limiting it to lunch or snack-time. It's great for breakfast, too!

PER SERVING (entire recipe): 230 calories, 4.5g fat, 808mg sodium, 34g carbs, 6.5g fiber, 9.5g sugars, 17g protein

o Ingredients

2 tablespoons low-fat marinara sauce
1 light English muffin, split into halves
1 stick light string cheese
2 slices shaved deli ham (honey or regular), chopped
1 pineapple ring packed in juice, drained and chopped
1 tablespoon chopped red onion

o Directions

Preheat oven to 350 degrees.

Spread 1 tablespoon sauce onto each muffin half.

Tear string cheese into shreds and roughly chop. Distribute cheese evenly over muffin halves. Top each half with ham, pineapple, and onion.

Extra, Extra!

Left with an open can of pineapple? Check out the Island Insanity Burger on page 130 and the Crazy Pineapple Salmon Teriyaki on page 154!

Place muffin halves on a baking sheet sprayed lightly with nonstick spray. Bake in the oven for 8 to 10 minutes. YUM!!!

MAKES 1 SERVING

 For a pic of this recipe, see the first photo insert. Yay!

am apple scramble

This isn't your average morning meal, people. It's got a whole slew of interesting and delicious stuff in it, and it tastes like scrambled French toast. Yum!

PER SERVING (entire scramble): 242 calories, 1.75g fat, 655mg sodium, 42g carbs, 6.25g fiber, 15.5g sugars, 17.5g protein

o Ingredients

1 slice light white bread
½ cup fat-free liquid egg substitute
2 tablespoons light vanilla soymilk
¼ teaspoon vanilla extract
½ teaspoon cinnamon, or more to taste

2 no-calorie sweetener packets
2 dashes salt, or more to taste
1 cup peeled and finely chopped apple
3 tablespoons old-fashioned oats

o Directions

Toast bread. Set aside to cool.

In a bowl, combine egg substitute, soymilk, vanilla extract, cinnamon, sweetener, and salt. Stir in apple and oats. Set aside.

Roughly tear bread and place in a blender or food processor. Pulse until reduced to small pieces.

Add egg-apple mixture to the blender/food processor and pulse until just mixed. (Do not over-blend.)

Bring a skillet sprayed with nonstick spray to medium heat. Add mixture and prepare as you would scrambled eggs, stirring and cooking for about 5 minutes, until solid bits form and mixture is slightly browned.

If you like, season with more cinnamon and salt. Enjoy!

MAKES 1 SERVING

tremendous
top-shelf turkey burger

It's HUGE and scrumdiddlyumptious—and great on a plate or on a bun.

PER SERVING (entire recipe): 184 calories, 6.5g fat, 502mg sodium, 12g carbs, 2g fiber, 4g sugars, 20.5g protein

○ Ingredients

½ slice light white bread
3 ounces raw lean ground turkey
¼ cup finely chopped mushrooms
3 tablespoons finely chopped onion
1 tablespoon fat-free liquid egg substitute

½ tablespoon finely chopped parsley
½ tablespoon Dijonnaise
½ tablespoon ketchup
¼ teaspoon crushed garlic
Dash salt

○ Directions

Place bread in a blender or food processor, and pulse until you have soft, fluffy breadcrumbs.

In a bowl, combine breadcrumbs with all other ingredients, and knead by hand until integrated. Form into a nice, big patty about ¾-inch thick.

Bring a skillet or grill pan sprayed with nonstick spray to medium heat. Place patty in the skillet/grill pan, cover, and cook for 5 to 7 minutes per side, until patty is cooked through. (Pssst . . . flip carefully.)

Serve on a plate, on a bun, over lettuce . . . whatever!

MAKES 1 SERVING

outside-in cheeseburger patty

We've boldly placed Laughing Cow wedges where they've never been placed before. We're adventurous like that.

> **PER SERVING** (entire recipe): 179 calories, 6.5g fat, 502mg sodium, 1.5g carbs, 0g fiber, 1g sugars, 26.5g protein

○ Ingredients

4 ounces raw extra-lean ground beef
⅛ teaspoon garlic powder
⅛ teaspoon onion powder
⅛ teaspoon Worcestershire sauce

Dash salt, or more to taste
Dash black pepper, or more to taste
1 wedge The Laughing Cow Light Original
    Swiss cheese

○ Directions

Combine all ingredients except cheese in a bowl. Add as much salt and pepper as you like. Knead mixture by hand until integrated.

Form into a ball and, using your thumb, make a large, hollow indentation in the ball (past the center but not all the way through). Fill the hole with cheese and squeeze the meat to seal, making sure no cheese is exposed. Flatten slightly into a thick patty.

Bring a skillet or grill pan sprayed with nonstick spray to medium-high heat. Place patty in the skillet/grill pan, cover, and cook for 4 to 7 minutes per side, depending on how well done you like your burger. Heads Up: Don't press on the patty with your spatula (your burger might ooze cheese!).

Serve however you like your burger . . . We like ours with ketchup and pickles between giant leaves of lettuce!

MAKES 1 SERVING

cheesy green eggs 'n hamwiches

Do not fear eggs that have a green hue. They're just, um, different. Heads up: If you use egg whites instead of (yellow) egg substitute, your eggs will be alarmingly green. Consider yourself warned. (Pssst . . . Kids LOVE this recipe!)

PER SERVING (entire recipe): 255 calories, 4.5g fat, 1,319mg sodium, 25g carbs, 5.75g fiber, 3g sugars, 30g protein

o Ingredients

1 light English muffin, split into halves
2 ounces (about 4 slices) 97 to 98% fat-free ham
½ cup fat-free liquid egg substitute
2 drops green food coloring
1 wedge The Laughing Cow Light Original Swiss cheese
Optional: salt

o Directions

Toast muffin halves until they're as crispy as you like. Place ham in a large microwave-safe mug, and microwave just until warm, about 20 seconds. Evenly top muffin halves with ham, and then set aside.

Spray the microwave-safe mug lightly with nonstick spray. Add egg substitute, food coloring, and cheese wedge, breaking cheese into pieces as you add it. Mix well.

Microwave for 1 minute. Stir and microwave for an additional 45 to 60 seconds, until fully cooked. Stir again.

Evenly distribute eggs between the ham-topped muffin halves. If you like, sprinkle with some salt. Enjoy!

MAKES 1 SERVING

smothered pepperoni pizza breakfast burrito

For serious foodies who know it's never too early in the day to enjoy delicious, saucy, cheesy, pizza goodness.

> **PER SERVING** (entire burrito): 284 calories, 6.5g fat, 1,078mg sodium, 31g carbs, 7.5g fiber, 4.5g sugars, 30g protein

o Ingredients

½ cup fat-free liquid egg substitute
2 tablespoons chopped green bell pepper
1 tablespoon chopped onion
1 burrito-size flour tortilla with about 110 calories
2 tablespoons diced tomatoes
Dash garlic powder, or more to taste

Dash black pepper
6 slices turkey pepperoni, halved
1 stick light string cheese
3 tablespoons canned crushed tomatoes
1 teaspoon reduced-fat Parmesan-style grated topping
Optional: salt

o Directions

Preheat oven to 350 degrees.

Spray a large microwave-safe mug with nonstick spray. Add egg substitute, bell pepper, and onion, and microwave for 1 minute.

Stir gently, and then microwave for another 45 to 60 seconds, until scramble is just set.

Warm tortilla for about 10 seconds in the microwave. Spread diced tomatoes down the center of the tortilla, and sprinkle with garlic powder and black pepper. Top with turkey pepperoni, followed by egg scramble.

Tear string cheese into shreds and place on top of the eggs. Wrap tortilla up like a burrito, folding the sides in first, and then rolling it up from the bottom.

Place burrito seam-side down on a baking sheet sprayed with nonstick spray, and bake in the oven for 8 to 10 minutes, until crispy. Meanwhile, place crushed tomatoes in a microwave-safe bowl and heat in the microwave. If you like, season to taste with garlic powder and salt.

Plate your burrito and top with crushed tomatoes and grated topping. Enjoy!

MAKES 1 SERVING

For Weight Watchers *POINTS*®
values and photos of all the
recipes in this book, check out
hungry-girl.com/book.

totally thai chicken lettuce cups

Just like the stuff you find at your favorite restaurants—without all the hidden calories and fat grams. SCORE!

PER SERVING (entire recipe): 227 calories, 4.5g fat, 875mg sodium, 21g carbs, 3g fiber, 12.5g sugars, 23g protein

○ Ingredients

¾ cup peeled and diced cucumber
2 scallions, cut into ½-inch pieces
2 tablespoons shredded carrot
2 tablespoons seasoned rice vinegar
1 tablespoon chopped cilantro
Dash crushed red pepper, or more to taste
3 ounces raw boneless skinless lean
    chicken breast, cubed

⅛ teaspoon garlic powder
1½ tablespoons Thai peanut salad
    dressing or sauce (low in fat with
    about 35 calories per tablespoon)
3 leaves romaine, butter, or green leaf lettuce
Optional garnishes: lime wedges,
    sesame seeds

○ Directions

In a bowl, combine cucumber, scallions, carrot shreds, rice vinegar, cilantro, and crushed red pepper. Mix well and refrigerate until you're ready to assemble your cups.

Bring a skillet sprayed with nonstick spray to medium-high heat. Add chicken and sprinkle with garlic powder. Cook chicken, stirring occasionally, until browned and cooked through, about 4 minutes.

Place chicken and peanut dressing or sauce in a bowl and toss to coat. Remove veggie mixture from the fridge.

To assemble, evenly distribute the veggie mixture and the chicken among the lettuce "cups." If you like, finish with a squirt of lime juice and a sprinkle of sesame seeds. Chomp chomp!

MAKES 1 SERVING

lucky four-leaf salad with feta and apples

Ooooh, look at us. We've created a classy, refreshing, and totally guilt-free salad with fruit and cheese. Yay!

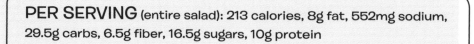

PER SERVING (entire salad): 213 calories, 8g fat, 552mg sodium, 29.5g carbs, 6.5g fiber, 16.5g sugars, 10g protein

Ingredients

1 Fuji apple
3 cups 3-lettuce blend bagged lettuce
1 cup spinach leaves
¼ cup crumbled reduced-fat feta cheese
¼ cup thinly sliced red onion
1 tablespoon thinly sliced dry-roasted almonds
Optional: freshly ground black pepper, light
　　　vinaigrette dressing or
　　　another low-calorie dressing

Directions

Cut apple into quarters and remove the core, seeds, and stem. Thinly slice, and then cut the slices in half widthwise.

Toss all ingredients together in a bowl. Add some pepper and dressing if you like, but this salad's so flavorful you may not even need 'em. Enjoy!!!

MAKES 1 SERVING

honey mustard
pretzel-coated chicken fingers

Confession time! I'm a little obsessed with these. They actually remind me of the little Weaver chicken drummies I ate when I was a kid. They had bones back then, and weren't made with pretzels, and were actually NOTHING like these. But the sweet, salty flavor of this recipe is reminiscent of those little drummettes . . . and I LOVE IT!!!

> **PER SERVING** (entire recipe): 349 calories, 2.5g fat, 928mg sodium, 39g carbs, 1g fiber, 13.5g sugars, 37g protein

o Ingredients

3 tablespoons honey mustard

2 tablespoons fat-free liquid egg substitute

5 ounces raw boneless skinless lean chicken breast, cut into 4 strips

2 dashes salt

2 dashes black pepper

1 ounce (about 10 twists) hard salted pretzels, finely crushed

2 teaspoons granulated sugar

o Directions

Preheat oven to 375 degrees.

Mix honey mustard and egg substitute together in a small bowl. Season chicken strips with salt and pepper, and then submerge in the mustard-egg mixture. Set aside to marinate for at least 5 minutes.

Mix crushed pretzels with sugar and spread mixture out on a plate. Spray a baking sheet with nonstick spray.

Thoroughly coat chicken strips with the pretzel-sugar mixture, and then transfer to the baking sheet. (Discard excess mustard-egg mixture.) Mist the tops of the strips with nonstick spray.

Bake in the oven for about 20 minutes, flipping chicken halfway through baking, until chicken is cooked through.

Eat and enjoy!

MAKES 1 SERVING

santa fe cheesy chicken stir-fry

Love cheese, chicken, and southwestern flavors? Let the stir-frying begin!

PER SERVING (entire recipe): 256 calories, 2g fat, 693mg sodium, 19.5g carbs, 3.25g fiber, 4.5g sugars, 38.5g protein

○ Ingredients

4 ounces raw boneless skinless lean chicken breast, chopped
2 tablespoons canned black beans, drained and rinsed
½ tablespoon chopped cilantro
½ teaspoon lime juice
⅛ teaspoon chili powder
⅛ teaspoon salt

2 dashes ground cumin
2 dashes black pepper
¼ cup frozen corn
¼ cup thinly sliced onion
¼ cup thinly sliced red bell pepper
¼ cup shredded fat-free cheddar cheese
¼ cup chopped tomatoes

○ Directions

In a bowl, combine chicken, beans, cilantro, lime juice, chili powder, salt, cumin, and black pepper. Mix well and set aside.

Bring a skillet sprayed with nonstick spray to medium-high heat. Add corn, onion, and bell pepper. Stirring frequently, cook for 4 to 5 minutes, until onion softens.

Extra, Extra!

Got black beans? Whip up the Bursting Burrito Bowl (page 136) or the Fiesta Bites (page 252)!

Add chicken mixture and, stirring occasionally, cook for 5 minutes, or until chicken is cooked through.

Add cheese and tomatoes and stir until cheese starts to melt. Enjoy immediately!

MAKES 1 SERVING

totally terrific tuna melt

The perfect tuna salad is easier than you think. Just swap out the usual fatty mix-ins for pickles, onions, and fat-free Greek yogurt. SO SIMPLE!

> **PER SERVING** (entire recipe): 298 calories, 3g fat, 1,379mg sodium, 31.5g carbs, 6.25g fiber, 4g sugars, 39g protein

o Ingredients

1 light English muffin, split into halves
3 ounces (about 1/3 cup) albacore tuna
    packed in water, drained and flaked
1 tablespoon Dijonnaise
1 tablespoon fat-free plain Greek yogurt
½ tablespoon chopped dill pickle

1 teaspoon dried minced onion
Squirt of lemon juice
Dash garlic powder
Dash black pepper
2 slices plum tomato
2 slices fat-free cheddar cheese

o Directions

Preheat broiler.

Lightly toast muffin halves. Set aside on a baking sheet lightly sprayed with nonstick spray.

In a small bowl, combine tuna, Dijonnaise, yogurt, pickle, onion, lemon juice, garlic powder, and pepper. Mix well.

Evenly distribute tuna mixture between the muffin halves. Top each with a slice of tomato followed by a slice of cheese.

Broil for 1 to 2 minutes, until cheese melts.

Plate your open-faced tuna melt and eat up!

MAKES 1 SERVING

HG Alternative!

Feel free to use fat-free mayo instead of Greek yogurt in this recipe.

pizza-fied chicken

Oooooh . . . This is like an oddly shaped pizza with chicken as the crust. So cool!

PER SERVING (entire recipe): 282 calories, 5.75g fat, 868mg sodium, 10g carbs, 2g fiber, 4.5g sugars, 44g protein

Ingredients

¼ cup canned crushed tomatoes
1 stick light string cheese
5 ounces raw boneless skinless lean
    chicken breast
¼ teaspoon garlic powder
¼ teaspoon onion powder
⅛ teaspoon salt, or more to taste
⅛ teaspoon black pepper, or more to taste

¼ cup diced green bell pepper
¼ cup sliced mushrooms
2 tablespoons diced onion
4 slices turkey pepperoni, chopped
1 teaspoon reduced-fat Parmesan-style
    grated topping
Optional seasonings and toppings: crushed
    red pepper, oregano, basil

Directions

Preheat broiler.

If you like, season crushed tomatoes to taste with salt, black pepper, and optional seasonings. Set aside. Tear string cheese into shreds, roughly chop, and set aside.

Place chicken in a large sealable plastic bag and, removing as much air as possible, seal the bag. Carefully pound chicken through the bag with a meat mallet or a heavy can, until it is uniformly about ½-inch thick. Evenly sprinkle both sides of the chicken with the garlic powder, onion powder, salt, and black pepper. Set aside.

Bring an oven-safe skillet sprayed with nonstick spray to medium heat on the stove. Add bell pepper, mushrooms, and onion and cook until softened, about 4 to 6 minutes. Remove veggies and set aside.

Remove skillet from heat, re-spray, and return to medium heat. Add chicken and cook for about 3 minutes per side, until cooked through.

Top chicken with crushed tomatoes, string cheese, veggies, and turkey pepperoni.

Place skillet under the broiler for 2 to 3 minutes, until cheese softens and pepperoni becomes crisp.

Plate your pizza-fied chicken and sprinkle with grated topping. If you like, sprinkle with optional toppings. Enjoy!

MAKES 1 SERVING

HG Tip!

If you're not sure if the handle of your skillet is oven-safe, wrap the handle with aluminum foil before heating it.

chop-chop beef stir-fry

Tastes like delicious takeout with way fewer calories and fat grams. It's sweet, spicy, and REALLY tasty!

> **PER SERVING** (entire recipe): 293 calories, 6.5g fat, 759mg sodium, 26g carbs, 7.5g fiber, 7g sugars, 35g protein

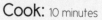 Ingredients

½ cup fat-free beef broth
½ tablespoon reduced-sodium/lite
    soy sauce
½ tablespoon cornstarch
4 ounces raw lean beefsteak filet, sliced
½ tablespoon chopped garlic

¼ teaspoon crushed red pepper
2 cups broccoli florets
1 cup sugar snap peas
1 cup sliced mushrooms
2 tablespoons chopped scallions
Optional: salt

Directions

Combine beef broth, soy sauce, and cornstarch in a bowl, and mix until cornstarch dissolves. Add beef, garlic, and crushed red pepper. Toss to coat and let marinate in the fridge for 10 minutes.

Bring a skillet sprayed with nonstick spray to medium-high heat. Add broccoli, sugar snap peas, mushrooms, scallions, and ¼ cup of the marinade from the beef. Cook for about 5 minutes, stirring occasionally, until broccoli softens.

Add beef and remaining marinade, and cook until browned and cooked through, about 3 minutes.

Reduce heat to low, cover, and let simmer for 2 minutes.

Serve it up and, if you like, season to taste with salt. Enjoy!

MAKES 1 SERVING

too-beautiful turkey burger

This swap for the Ruby Tuesday classic has Swiss cheese, sautéed mushrooms, and more. Plus, it saves you a ridiculous amount of fat and calories. Go, us!

> **PER SERVING** (entire recipe): 305 calories, 11.5g fat, 578mg sodium, 22g carbs, 4g fiber, 4g sugars, 32g protein

o Ingredients

1 small light hamburger bun (about 80 calories)
2 small lettuce leaves
2 slices tomato
1 raw plain lean turkey burger patty
1 slice 2% milk Swiss cheese
½ cup sliced baby bella mushrooms
Optional: pickles, ketchup, mustard

o Directions

Split bun in half, and toast lightly. Place lettuce and tomato on the bottom half of the bun. If you like, add a few pickle chips, a squirt of ketchup, and some mustard. Set aside.

Cook turkey patty in a skillet or grill pan sprayed with nonstick spray (refer to packaging for specific time and cooking temperature).

Once cooked, place patty on the bottom half of the bun, and immediately top with cheese.

Remove skillet/grill pan from heat and re-spray with nonstick spray. Over medium heat, cook mushroom slices until tender, about 3 minutes, stirring occasionally.

Place mushrooms over the cheese-topped patty. Top with the other half of the bun and enjoy!

MAKES 1 SERVING

📷 For a pic of this recipe, see the first photo insert. Yay!

HG Alternative!

Can't find 80-calorie buns? No worries! Get the lowest-calorie ones you can find, and adjust the nutritionals for this recipe accordingly.

bowling for pizza

Fun, filling, unique, and delicious. We'll take our pizza any way we can, and this one has no crust! Cool, huh?

> **PER SERVING** (entire bowl): 284 calories, 7g fat, 1,025mg sodium, 28.5g carbs, 9.25g fiber, 11g sugars, 30.5g protein

○ Ingredients

⅓ cup canned crushed tomatoes
1 stick light string cheese
1 cup sliced mushrooms
1 cup sliced green bell pepper
½ cup sliced onion
1 Boca Original Meatless Burger (Vegan), thawed and chopped

½ cup diced tomatoes
1 teaspoon reduced-fat Parmesan-style grated topping
8 slices turkey pepperoni, chopped
1 tablespoon sliced black olives
Optional: salt, black pepper, garlic powder, onion powder, crushed red pepper

○ Directions

If you like, season crushed tomatoes to taste with optional ingredients. Set aside. Tear string cheese into shreds, roughly chop, and set aside.

In a skillet sprayed with nonstick spray, cook mushrooms, bell pepper, and onion over medium heat until softened, about 3 to 5 minutes.

Add chopped Boca patty, diced tomatoes, and crushed tomatoes, and continue cooking until heated through, about 3 minutes.

Transfer to a microwave-safe bowl and immediately sprinkle with string cheese, grated topping, turkey pepperoni, and olives.

Microwave for about 30 seconds, just long enough to heat and soften the cheese. Enjoy!!!

MAKES 1 SERVING

For more recipes, tips & tricks, food finds, and MORE, sign up for FREE daily emails at hungry-girl.com!

6 Points + pasta

sausage, peppers, and onions italia

Try this decadent Italian classic served over Tofu Shirataki noodles for added chewing fun.

> **PER SERVING** (entire recipe): 295 calories, 8.25g fat, 905mg sodium, 35g carbs, 7.25g fiber, 18g sugars, 22g protein

o Ingredients

½ cup canned crushed tomatoes

1 teaspoon dried oregano

½ teaspoon garlic powder

1¼ cups thickly sliced onion

1½ cups thickly sliced red and green bell peppers

1 precooked 3-ounce chicken or meatless sausage link with 8g fat or less, sliced into ½-inch rounds

Optional: salt and black pepper

o Directions

Combine crushed tomatoes, oregano, and garlic powder in a bowl, and stir well. Set aside.

Bring a skillet sprayed with nonstick spray to medium-high heat. Add onion and cook for 2 minutes. Add bell peppers and continue to cook, stirring occasionally, for 2 to 4 minutes, until veggies are slightly softened.

Add sausage and cook for an additional 1 to 2 minutes, until heated.

Add tomatoes and stir. Once heated, season to taste with salt and black pepper (or not). Now chew!

MAKES 1 SERVING

HG Tip!

If using frozen sausage, do not thaw completely. This will make it easier to slice.

chapter two

Fast &
for Two
(or Three,
or Four!)

Hooray, you're FINALLY cooking for more than one person!

Here are some super-delicious multi-serving recipes.

three-cheese
bacon-apple-bella frittata

Bacon and apple and cheese and eggs?! Sounds like a fancy breakfast party to me!
Try serving this one up at brunch . . . or just keep it all for yourself!

> **PER SERVING** (¼ of frittata): 157 calories, 3.25g fat,
> 506mg sodium, 12.5g carbs, 1.5g fiber, 6.5g sugars, 18.5g protein

o Ingredients

1½ cups fat-free liquid egg substitute
2 tablespoons fat-free nondairy
    liquid creamer
2 slices 2% milk Swiss cheese, chopped
½ cup shredded fat-free cheddar cheese
2 slices center-cut bacon or turkey
    bacon, chopped

1 cup chopped portabella mushrooms
1 large apple (preferably Fuji), cored
    and finely chopped
1 tablespoon reduced-fat Parmesan-style
    grated topping

o Directions

Preheat broiler.

In a medium bowl, combine egg substitute and creamer. Whisk together for 1 minute. Add
Swiss cheese and cheddar cheese. Set aside.

Bring a large oven-safe skillet sprayed with nonstick spray to medium heat on the stove.

Add bacon and mushrooms, and cook until bacon is slightly crispy and mushrooms have softened, about 3 to 5 minutes.

Add apple and continue to cook until softened, about 2 minutes.

Pour egg mixture into the skillet, and tilt the skillet back and forth to ensure egg mixture is evenly distributed. Make sure cheese is evenly distributed, as well. If needed, run a spatula along the sides of the skillet to help egg to flow underneath the bacon, mushrooms, and apple. Cook for 2 minutes, and then remove from heat.

Sprinkle grated topping evenly over the frittata. Place under the broiler for about 4 minutes, until the egg mixture has puffed up and the mixture is set.

Allow to cool, and then cut into quarters. (Frittata may look runny, but it's just all the cheese oozing out!) Enjoy!

MAKES 4 SERVINGS

For a pic of this recipe, see the first photo insert. Yay!

HG Tip!

If you're not sure if the handle of your skillet is oven-safe, wrap the handle with aluminum foil before heating it.

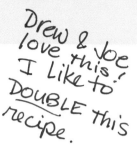

shrimp & grits . . . for hungry chicks!

Oh, Paula Deen—please forgive me for taking your beloved super-fattening-yet-incredibly-delicious recipe and HG-izing a bazillion calories and fat grams out of it. Pleeeeaze!?! By the way, it's STILL incredibly delicious.

> **PER SERVING** (½ of recipe): 380 calories, 8g fat, 900mg sodium, 40g carbs, 2.5g fiber, 1g sugars, 40g protein

○ Ingredients

½ cup quick-cooking grits
Dash salt
½ cup shredded fat-free cheddar cheese
1 tablespoon light whipped butter or light buttery spread
1 wedge The Laughing Cow Light Original Swiss cheese
8 ounces raw shrimp, peeled, tails removed, deveined

½ cup thinly sliced scallions (white and green parts)
1 tablespoon chopped fresh parsley
1 teaspoon lemon juice
½ teaspoon chopped garlic
2 tablespoons precooked real crumbled bacon
Optional: hot sauce

○ Directions

In a medium pot, bring 2 cups water to a boil on the stove. Add grits and salt and stir well. Reduce heat to lowest setting. Stirring occasionally, cook until water has been absorbed, about 6 to 7 minutes. Remove from heat and stir in shredded cheese, butter, and cheese wedge, breaking cheese wedge into pieces as you add it. Cover and set aside until ready to serve.

Bring a large skillet sprayed with nonstick spray to medium heat. Add shrimp and cook until opaque, about 3 minutes, flipping halfway through cooking. Add scallions, parsley, lemon juice, and garlic. If you like, add a dash or two of hot sauce. Stir well and remove from heat.

Serve grits topped with shrimp and bacon. Eat up, y'all!

MAKES 2 SERVINGS

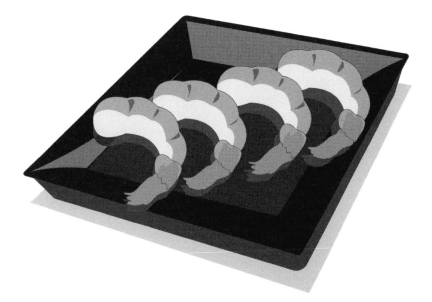 For a pic of this recipe, see the first photo insert. Yay!

amazin' asian ahi tuna burgers

You MUST use fresh ahi for these burgers. DON'T cut corners and attempt to make these with the frozen stuff. BTW, the wasabi mayo packs a fair amount of heat. Don't say I didn't warn you . . .

> **PER SERVING** (1 burger): 246 calories, 2.5g fat, 734mg sodium, 26.5g carbs, 3g fiber, 3.5g sugars, 33g protein

o Ingredients

⅓ cup fat-free mayonnaise

2 teaspoons wasabi, or less for a milder sauce

1 pound fresh raw ahi/yellowfin tuna, finely chopped

1 extra-large egg white or 3 tablespoons liquid egg whites

3 scallions, chopped

1½ tablespoons reduced-sodium/lite soy sauce

2 teaspoons ground ginger

1 teaspoon Dijon mustard

Dash black pepper

4 small light hamburger buns (about 80 calories each), toasted

1 small cucumber, thinly sliced

o Directions

In a small bowl, combine mayo and wasabi. Mix well and set aside.

In a medium bowl, combine tuna, egg white, scallions, soy sauce, ginger, mustard, and pepper. Mix well. Using your hands, shape mixture into 4 patties, each approximately 4 inches wide.

Spray a large skillet with nonstick spray and bring to medium-high heat. Place patties in the pan and cook until golden on the outside and medium-rare on the inside, about 2 minutes per side. (Be sure to flip them gently!)

Place each patty on the bottom half of a bun. Top each evenly with mayo-wasabi mixture. Finish each one off with cucumber slices and a top bun half!

MAKES 4 SERVINGS

HG Alternative!

Can't find 80-calorie buns? No worries! Get the lowest-calorie ones you can find, and adjust the nutritionals for this recipe accordingly.

For Weight Watchers *POINTS*® values and photos of all the recipes in this book, check out hungry-girl.com/book.

good chick lollipops

Please admire the clever use of Funyuns in this recipe. Funyuns = good times. And don't you forget it . . .

> **PER SERVING** (2 "lollipops"): 196 calories, 3.5g fat, 315mg sodium, 10.5g carbs, 0.5g fiber, 0.5g sugars, 28g protein

○ Ingredients

12 ounces raw boneless skinless lean chicken breasts, cut into 6 strips

1 ounce (about 15 pieces) Funyuns Onion Flavored Rings

½ ounce (about 7 chips) fat-free sour cream & onion potato chips

1 teaspoon onion powder, or more to taste

2 dashes garlic powder, or more to taste

2 dashes salt, or more to taste

⅛ teaspoon black pepper

2 tablespoons fat-free liquid egg substitute

○ Directions

Preheat oven to 375 degrees.

Carefully slide each chicken strip lengthwise onto a skewer. Set aside.

In a large sealable plastic bag, combine Funyuns, potato chips, and all the seasonings. If you like, add extra seasonings to taste. Seal the bag and crush contents until reduced to a coarse breadcrumb-like consistency. Transfer to a plate and set aside.

Prepare a large baking sheet by spraying with nonstick spray. Pour egg substitute into a small bowl.

Take a chicken skewer and dunk it in the egg substitute—use a spoon to evenly coat the chicken. Gently shake to remove any excess liquid, and then lay chicken skewer in the seasoned crumbs. Rotate the skewer, pressing it into the crumbs, until it is evenly coated. Use your fingers or a spoon to add and pat crumbs onto any bare spots on the chicken. Transfer to the baking sheet, and repeat with all other chicken skewers.

Bake in the oven for 18 to 20 minutes, carefully flipping skewers about halfway through cooking, until chicken is cooked through and coating is crispy. Allow to cool for a few minutes, and then enjoy!

MAKES 3 SERVINGS

HG Tip!

If using wooden skewers, make sure to soak 'em in water for 20 to 30 minutes first to keep 'em from burning.

spring chicken skillet

Here's a classic dish to add to your portfolio of chicken recipes. This one's a keeper!

> **PER SERVING** (1/3rd of recipe, about 1 1/3 cups): 202 calories, 2g fat, 414mg sodium, 8g carbs, 1.5g fiber, 4g sugars, 36g protein

○ Ingredients

1 pound raw boneless skinless lean chicken breasts
½ tablespoon dry chicken grill seasoning blend

1 onion, chopped
1 tablespoon chopped garlic
2 cups cherry tomatoes
¼ teaspoon salt

○ Directions

Sprinkle chicken on both sides with grill seasoning blend. Bring a large skillet sprayed with nonstick spray to medium-high heat. Add chicken and cook for 3 to 4 minutes on each side, until seared. Remove chicken and, once cool enough to handle, chop into bite-sized pieces.

Remove skillet from heat, re-spray with nonstick spray, and return to medium-high heat. Add chopped chicken, onion, and garlic to the skillet, and cook until onions are browned and chicken is fully cooked, about 5 minutes. Add tomatoes and salt, and stir.

Reduce heat to low, cover skillet, and let simmer for 8 to 10 minutes, until the tomatoes burst.

Using a spatula, carefully mash any tomatoes that have yet to burst. Gently scrape up onion and garlic bits from the bottom of the skillet and mix them up with the juice from the tomatoes. Stir well and serve!

MAKES 3 SERVINGS

For a pic of this recipe, see the first photo insert. Yay!

fiesta noodle casserole

HG subscriber Susan is the brilliant human who inspired this recipe. It's pretty awesome, and the serving size is tremendous. I love that in a recipe . . .

> **PER SERVING** (¼ of casserole): 105 calories, 1.5g fat, 612mg sodium, 11g carbs, 5g fiber, 2g sugars, 12.5g protein

o Ingredients

3 packages House Foods Tofu Shirataki Fettuccine Shaped Noodle Substitute

1½ cups ground-beef-style soy crumbles, thawed from frozen

½ cup red taco sauce

2 teaspoons dry taco seasoning mix

¼ cup plus 2 tablespoons shredded fat-free cheddar cheese

Optional: fat-free sour cream

o Directions

Preheat oven to 375 degrees.

Use a strainer to rinse and drain shirataki noodles well. Pat dry. In a large microwave-safe bowl, microwave for 1 minute. Drain excess liquid. Dry as thoroughly as possible, using paper towels. Cut noodles up a bit.

Add crumbles, taco sauce, and taco seasoning, and mix well.

Transfer mixture to a baking dish sprayed with nonstick spray. Sprinkle with cheese, and then bake in the oven for 20 to 25 minutes, until bubbly.

Top each serving with a dollop of sour cream, if you like. Enjoy!

MAKES 4 SERVINGS

You'll Need: bowl, 4 skewers, nonstick spray, grill, long barbecue tongs
Marinate: at least 1 hour   **Cook:** 15 minutes

chicken d'lish kebabs

Make sure you read the title of this recipe correctly. Say it all at once—it rhymes with "shish kebabs." DO IT! D'lish Kebabs. Seeeee . . . isn't that fun?!?!

> **PER SERVING** (2 kebabs): 285 calories, 3g fat, 432mg sodium, 21.5g carbs, 5g fiber, 12g sugars, 44g protein

○ Ingredients

¼ cup plain fat-free yogurt
1 teaspoon lemon juice
¼ teaspoon curry powder
¼ teaspoon garlic powder
¼ teaspoon onion powder
¼ teaspoon salt

Dash paprika
12 ounces raw boneless skinless lean chicken
    breasts, cut into 1½-inch cubes
2 red bell peppers
1 large (or 2 small) yellow summer squash
1 onion

○ Directions

In a medium bowl, combine yogurt, lemon juice, and all seasonings. Stir well. Add chicken and coat completely. Cover and refrigerate for at least 1 hour.

Meanwhile, cut bell peppers, squash, and onion into chunks equal in size to the chicken cubes.

Skewer the chicken and veggies alternately onto four skewers, packing the pieces together tightly.

Spray grill lightly with nonstick spray, and bring to medium-high heat.

Grill kebabs for 5 minutes with the grill cover down. Then carefully flip kebabs with long barbecue tongs.

With the grill cover down, grill for another 5 to 7 minutes, until chicken is cooked through.

Remove from grill and allow to cool slightly. Once cool enough to handle, pull chicken and veggies off the sticks and eat!

MAKES 2 SERVINGS

HG Tip!

If using wooden skewers, make sure to soak 'em in water for 20 to 30 minutes first to keep 'em from burning.

For more recipes, tips & tricks, food finds, and MORE, sign up for FREE daily emails at hungry-girl.com!

planet hungrywood
sweet & cap'n crunchy chicken

I spent too many hours in the '90s chewing on a version of this served at Planet Hollywood, likely a fattening one. I finally decided it was time to give it up, and I hadn't thought about it for roughly a decade . . . until it occurred to me that I could create a guilt-free swap pretty easily. Here it is. Even the Cap'n himself would be proud!

> **PER SERVING** (½ of recipe): 234 calories, 2g fat, 617mg sodium, 23.5g carbs, 4g fiber, 10g sugars, 29g protein

o Ingredients

¼ cup Fiber One bran cereal (original)
½ cup Cap'n Crunch cereal (original)
⅛ teaspoon onion powder
⅛ teaspoon garlic powder
Dash salt
Dash black pepper

8 ounces raw boneless skinless lean chicken breast, cut into 4 strips
3 tablespoons fat-free liquid egg substitute
2 tablespoons Dijonnaise
2 tablespoons honey mustard

o Directions

Place Fiber One in a blender or food processor, and grind to a breadcrumb-like consistency. Set aside.

Place Cap'n Crunch in a sealable plastic bag and seal. Using a rolling pin or a heavy can, coarsely crush cereal. In a wide bowl, combine Fiber One crumbs, crushed Cap'n Crunch, and all seasonings. Mix well and set aside.

54

Place chicken strips in a separate bowl. Pour egg substitute over the chicken strips, and flip to coat. Shake off any excess egg substitute, and then coat chicken strips in the cereal mixture.

Bring a large skillet sprayed with nonstick spray to medium heat on the stove. Place coated chicken strips gently into the skillet, spacing them out as much as possible. Cook for 5 minutes, and then carefully flip pieces over. Cook for about 4 additional minutes, until chicken is cooked through.

Combine the Dijonnaise and honey mustard in a small bowl, and mix well for a tasty dipping sauce. Enjoy!

MAKES 2 SERVINGS

 For a pic of this recipe, see the first photo insert. Yay!

aloha under the sea

It's a Hawaiian-inspired, sweet 'n sassy seafood extravaganza. Weeeeee!

> **PER SERVING** (¼th of recipe, about 1½ cups): 286 calories, 3g fat, 777mg sodium, 38g carbs, 2.5g fiber, 26g sugars, 25.5g protein

o Ingredients

¼ cup ketchup

1½ tablespoons reduced-sodium/lite soy sauce

1 tablespoon brown sugar (not packed)

1 tablespoon cornstarch

1 tablespoon dry onion soup mix

2 teaspoons Dijonnaise

1 teaspoon chopped garlic

One 20-ounce can pineapple chunks in juice, not drained

6 ounces raw scallops, halved if large

6 ounces raw swordfish, cut into 1-inch cubes

1 sweet onion, thinly sliced

1 red bell pepper, thinly sliced

1 yellow or orange bell pepper, thinly sliced

6 ounces raw shrimp, peeled, tails removed, deveined

o Directions

Pour ½ cup water into a large pot. Add ketchup, soy sauce, brown sugar, cornstarch, onion soup mix, Dijonnaise, and garlic. Stir thoroughly, ensuring cornstarch dissolves.

Add pineapple, scallops, and swordfish, and set stove to medium heat. Stirring occasionally, cook for 8 minutes.

Add veggies and cook for 2 minutes. Add shrimp and, stirring occasionally, cook until shrimp are opaque and cooked through and sauce has thickened slightly, about 3 minutes.

Remove from heat and let stand for 5 minutes. (Sauce will thicken upon standing.)

Serve it up and dive in!

MAKES 4 SERVINGS

girl-on-grill veggie wraps

These wraps are an explosion of flavor. The fresh basil is soooo awesome in this recipe. Don't even THINK about trying to swap it out for the dried stuff. I'll be REALLY upset with you. Don't make me come over there . . .

> **PER SERVING** (1 wrap): 173 calories, 2.5g fat, 483mg sodium, 34.5g carbs, 10.5g fiber, 8.5g sugars, 10g protein

o Ingredients

Two ½-inch-thick peeled eggplant slices (cut lengthwise)

1 large portabella mushroom cap

1 red bell pepper, halved, seeds removed

1 small zucchini, ends removed, cut lengthwise into 4 slices

3 tablespoons plain fat-free yogurt

1 tablespoon finely chopped fresh basil

½ teaspoon crushed garlic

2 burrito-size flour tortillas with about 110 calories each

2 dashes salt

2 dashes black pepper

o Directions

Spray grill well with nonstick spray, and bring to medium-high heat.

Grill all the veggies for 5 minutes with the grill cover down. Then carefully flip with long barbecue tongs.

Grill veggies for about 5 minutes longer with the grill cover down, until slightly soft and blackened. Remove from grill and allow to cool slightly.

Meanwhile, in a small dish, combine yogurt, basil, and garlic, and mix well. Set aside.

Once veggies are cool enough to handle, cut mushroom cap and pepper halves into slices. Then warm tortillas slightly in the microwave (or carefully and quickly on the grill).

Spread half of the yogurt mixture onto each tortilla. Place a slice of eggplant down the center of each tortilla, and place a slice of zucchini on either side. Sprinkle with salt and black pepper.

Evenly distribute mushroom and pepper slices between the two tortillas, laying them in the same direction as the other veggie slices. Roll each tortilla up like a burrito.

Slice wraps in half (or don't) and enjoy!

MAKES 2 SERVINGS

For a pic of this recipe, see the first photo insert. Yay!

pan-fried chicken parm

Everyone will LOVE this super-easy, cheesy, no-guilt Italian favorite. (Though your Italian great-aunt might resist at first!)

> **PER SERVING** (½ of recipe): 258 calories, 6g fat, 684mg sodium, 16.5g carbs, 7g fiber, 1g sugars, 38.5g protein

o Ingredients

Two 4-ounce raw boneless skinless
  lean chicken breast cutlets
½ cup Fiber One bran cereal (original)
1½ teaspoons Italian seasoning, or
  more to taste
½ teaspoon garlic powder, divided, or
  more to taste
½ teaspoon onion powder, divided, or
  more to taste

⅛ teaspoon salt, or more to taste
¼ cup canned tomato sauce with
  Italian seasonings
¼ cup fat-free liquid egg substitute
½ cup shredded reduced-fat
  mozzarella cheese
Optional: Black pepper

o Directions

Place chicken in a large sealable plastic bag and, removing as much air as possible, seal the bag. Carefully pound chicken through the bag with a meat mallet or a heavy can, until it is uniformly about ½-inch thick.

Using a blender or food processor, grind Fiber One cereal to a breadcrumb-like consistency. In a medium bowl, combine "breadcrumbs" with Italian seasoning, ¼ teaspoon garlic powder, ¼ teaspoon onion powder, and salt. Feel free to season your breadcrumbs with as much pepper, additional salt, and additional spices as you like. Mix well.

In a small bowl, mix tomato sauce with remaining ¼ teaspoon garlic powder and ¼ teaspoon onion powder. Set aside.

Place egg substitute in a separate medium bowl. Coat raw chicken very well on both sides with the egg substitute. Then place chicken in the crumb mixture, and coat thoroughly on both sides.

Spray a large skillet with nonstick spray, and bring to medium-high heat. Place chicken in the skillet and cook for 4 minutes on each side, or until chicken is cooked through.

Once chicken is fully cooked, spread 2 tablespoons sauce over each cutlet, while chicken is still in the skillet. Evenly sprinkle cheese over the sauce-covered cutlets.

Reduce heat to low and cover skillet. Continue to cook for 2 to 3 minutes, until cheese has melted. Enjoy!!!

MAKES 2 SERVINGS

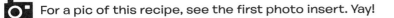 For a pic of this recipe, see the first photo insert. Yay!

veggie-rific fried rice

And you thought you had to give up fried rice forever. Silly you! This vegetabled-up version is good AND good for you. (Sorry to sound like a corny commercial from the '80s.) Enjoy!

> **PER SERVING** (1 cup): 167 calories, 0.5g fat, 630mg sodium, 30g carbs, 4g fiber, 4g sugars, 8.5g protein

○ Ingredients

One packet (about 1 ounce) dry fried
    rice seasoning mix
⅛ teaspoon garlic powder
⅛ teaspoon ground ginger
1 tablespoon reduced-sodium/lite soy sauce
¾ cup fat-free liquid egg substitute
2 cups frozen diced carrots and peas

1 cup chopped mushrooms
2 cups cooked brown rice,
    fridge temperature
1 cup chopped bean sprouts
¼ cup chopped scallions
Salt and black pepper, to taste

○ Directions

In a small dish, combine seasoning mix, garlic powder, and ground ginger with soy sauce and 3 tablespoons warm water. Stir until seasoning mix has dissolved. Set aside.

Spray a wok or very large skillet with nonstick spray, and bring it to medium heat. Add egg substitute and scramble until cooked, 2 to 3 minutes, using a spatula to break it up into bite-sized pieces. Remove scrambled bits from the wok/skillet and set aside.

Add frozen vegetables and mushrooms to the wok/skillet, and cook and stir until mushrooms have softened and all veggies are hot. Remove veggies and set aside with the egg-y bits.

Remove your wok/skillet from heat, re-spray with nonstick spray, and bring to high heat on the stove. Add rice and seasoning mixture, and stir to combine. Add bean sprouts, scallions, and the previously cooked veggies and scrambled eggs, and mix thoroughly to integrate. Cook and stir until entire mixture is hot, there is no liquid left in the skillet, and rice is just beginning to crisp. Season to taste with salt and pepper.

Scoop into bowls and serve! (Chopsticks not required.)

MAKES 5 SERVINGS

HG Heads Up!
Some fried rice seasoning mixes are not vegetarian-friendly, so read ingredients carefully if that's a concern.

te quiero tequila shrimp

Translated, this means, "I love you tequila shrimp," and that is 100 percent true. I DO love this tequila-infused shrimp. A lot. Like *a lot* a lot.

> **PER SERVING** (½ of recipe, about 1½ cups): 206 calories, 2.25g fat, 470mg sodium, 9.5g carbs, 1.75g fiber, 4g sugars, 24g protein

o Ingredients

1 small onion, sliced
1 teaspoon chopped garlic
3 tablespoons (1½ ounces or 1 shot) tequila
8 ounces raw shrimp, peeled, tails
    removed, deveined

2 Roma tomatoes, chopped
2 tablespoons lime juice
2 tablespoons coarsely chopped cilantro
¼ teaspoon chili powder
¼ teaspoon salt

o Directions

Bring a large skillet sprayed with nonstick spray to medium heat. Add onion and garlic, and cook until onion is slightly translucent, about 3 minutes. Carefully add tequila to the skillet and stir. (It's unlikely it will flare up, but be cautious, just in case.) Cover the skillet and let simmer for 5 minutes.

Add shrimp and cook for about 3 minutes, until shrimp are nearly opaque. Add tomatoes, lime juice, cilantro, chili powder, and salt, and mix well. Stirring occasionally, cook until tomatoes have softened and shrimp are opaque and cooked through, about 2 minutes. Enjoy!

MAKES 2 SERVINGS

 For a pic of this recipe, see the first photo insert. Yay!

devil-icious shrimp

Holy hot 'n spicy shrimp! This is one of my favorite recipes in the book. The portion size is HUGE, and it packs the perfect amount of heat. I love, love, LOVE this dish . . .

> **PER SERVING** (¼th of recipe, about 1½ cups): 208 calories, 2.5g fat, 736mg sodium, 19g carbs, 3.5g fiber, 10.5g sugars, 26g protein

o Ingredients

1 pound raw shrimp, peeled, tails removed, deveined
1 tablespoon chopped garlic
½ teaspoon crushed red pepper, or more to taste
1 onion, finely chopped

1 red bell pepper, chopped
1¾ cup canned crushed tomatoes with basil
One 14.5-ounce can fire-roasted diced tomatoes with garlic, drained
2 teaspoons dried oregano
½ teaspoon Frank's RedHot Original Cayenne Pepper Sauce, or more to taste
Optional: salt and black pepper

o Directions

Bring a medium-large pot sprayed well with nonstick spray to medium-low heat. Add shrimp, garlic, and crushed red pepper. Stirring occasionally, cook just until shrimp are opaque, about 1 to 2 minutes. Remove shrimp and set aside.

Add onion and bell pepper to the pot and raise heat to medium. Stirring occasionally, cook until softened, about 3 minutes.

Return the shrimp to the pot along with all other ingredients and mix well. Stirring occasionally, cook until sauce is hot and shrimp are cooked through, about 3 to 5 minutes.

Serve and, if you like, season to taste with additional crushed red pepper, additional hot sauce, and/or black pepper. Enjoy!

MAKES 4 SERVINGS

chicken enchilada casserole

This is one of those dishes that is practically IMPOSSIBLE to believe is low in calories and fat grams. It's crazy-decadent comfort food. Cheesy, saucy, creamy ... AHHHHHHHHHHHHH, IT'S SO GOOD! Sorry, almost lost it there.

> **PER SERVING** (¼ of casserole): 260 calories, 4g fat, 1,166mg sodium, 27g carbs, 4g fiber, 3g sugars, 27.5g protein

o Ingredients

One 9.75-ounce (or 10-ounce) can 98% fat-free chunk white chicken breast in water, drained and flaked

One 10.75-ounce can 98% fat-free cream of celery condensed soup

⅔ cup frozen bite-sized mixed veggies

½ cup salsa

Six 6-inch corn tortillas

1 cup shredded fat-free cheddar cheese, divided

Optional: salt and black pepper

o Directions

Preheat oven to 350 degrees.

In a large bowl, combine chicken, soup, veggies, and salsa. If you like, add salt and pepper. Mix well and set aside.

Spray a baking dish with nonstick spray. Break tortillas into pieces about the size of tortilla chips. Lay half of the tortilla pieces along the bottom of the baking dish.

Evenly layer half of the chicken mixture over the tortilla pieces. Sprinkle with ½ cup cheese. Lay remaining tortilla pieces over the cheese. Top evenly with the rest of the chicken mixture, followed by the remaining ½ cup cheese.

Bake in the oven for 35 minutes, or until edges are brown and crispy.

Allow to cool for about 5 minutes, until sauce thickens. Eat up!

MAKES 4 SERVINGS

chapter three

Nuke It, Baby!

Let's break it down, in case the title of this chapter isn't clear enough.

All of the recipes here are prepared in a microwave. Conventional ovens, toaster ovens, convection ovens, and stoves need not apply. And if you're the type of person who believes fantastic-tasting food can't be made in a microwave oven, we hope you don't mind being wrong every now and then.

college breakfast burrito

You don't have to be in college to enjoy this fast and delicious breakfast. But it *is* easy enough to be whipped up in a dorm or the kitchenette in your office . . . basically any place with a microwave and a power outlet.

> **PER SERVING** (entire burrito): 295 calories, 5g fat, 1,212mg sodium, 35.5g carbs, 7g fiber, 7g sugars, 30g protein

○ Ingredients

⅓ cup frozen potatoes O'Brien
1 precooked 1-ounce turkey or meatless
    sausage breakfast link, chopped
1 teaspoon dried minced onion
½ cup fat-free liquid egg substitute

1 burrito-size flour tortilla with about
    110 calories
1 slice fat-free American cheese, halved
1 tablespoon ketchup
Optional: salt and black pepper

○ Directions

Spray a large microwave-safe mug lightly with nonstick spray. Add potatoes, sausage, onion, and 1 teaspoon water, and stir. Microwave for 1 minute. Once cool enough to handle, transfer potato mixture to a plate and set aside.

Lightly re-spray mug with nonstick spray. Add egg substitute and microwave for 1 minute. Stir gently and then microwave for another 45 to 60 seconds, until scramble is just set.

Extra, Extra!

Potatoes O'Brien aren't just meant for this burrito. Buy a bag and use it for making our Big Bowl of Breakfast (page 122) and Happy Camper Cheeseburger Crumble (page 156)!

Warm tortilla in the microwave for about 10 seconds. Place egg scramble in the center of the tortilla. If you like, sprinkle with salt and pepper. Top with potato-sausage mixture followed by cheese and ketchup.

Roll the tortilla up tightly around the filling. Enjoy!

MAKES 1 SERVING

📷 For a pic of this recipe, see the first photo insert. Yay!

HG Tip!

If using frozen sausage, do not thaw completely. This will make it easier to chop.

egg mug florentine

You really can't say (or even read!) the word "Florentine" without feeling 20 percent fancier, can you? Despite that fact, this simple morning meal is down-to-earth and delicious!

PER SERVING (entire mug): 107 calories, 2g fat, 575mg sodium, 5g carbs, <0.5g fiber, 2.5g sugars, 15g protein

o Ingredients

1 teaspoon Dijonnaise
1 teaspoon plain fat-free yogurt
Squirt of lemon juice
½ cup chopped fresh spinach
½ cup fat-free liquid egg substitute
1 wedge The Laughing Cow Light Original Swiss cheese

o Directions

To make the sauce, stir to combine Dijonnaise, yogurt, and lemon juice in a small bowl. Set aside.

Spray a large microwave-safe mug lightly with nonstick spray. Add spinach and microwave for 30 seconds.

Blot excess liquid from spinach. Add egg substitute and cheese wedge, breaking cheese into pieces as you add it. Microwave for 1 minute.

Stir gently, and then microwave for another 45 to 60 seconds, until scramble is just set.

Stir scramble, top with sauce, and enjoy!

MAKES 1 SERVING

egg mug burger-rama

Fast food meets healthy breakfast meets your face (or the face of some other lucky human).

PER SERVING (entire mug): 175 calories, 0.5g fat, 995mg sodium, 14g carbs, 4g fiber, 6g sugars, 30g protein

○ Ingredients

1 Boca Original Meatless Burger (Vegan)
½ cup fat-free liquid egg substitute
1 slice fat-free American cheese, chopped
1 tablespoon ketchup

○ Directions

Microwave Boca patty for 1 minute, and then chop into pieces.

Spray a large microwave-safe mug lightly with nonstick spray. Add egg substitute, chopped Boca patty, and cheese, and stir. Microwave for 1 minute.

Stir gently, and then microwave for another 45 to 60 seconds, until scramble is just set.

Stir, top with ketchup, and enjoy!

MAKES 1 SERVING

egg mcmuggin'

You'll never hit the drive-thru for breakfast again. Never.

> **PER SERVING** (entire mug): 174 calories, 3.25g fat, 1,081mg sodium, 9g carbs, 1g fiber, 2.5g sugars, 25g protein

o Ingredients

½ slice light bread
½ cup fat-free liquid egg substitute
1½ ounces (about 3 slices) 97 to 98% fat-free ham, chopped
1 wedge The Laughing Cow Light Original Swiss cheese
1 tablespoon shredded fat-free cheddar cheese

o Directions

Toast bread, and then cut into cubes.

Spray a large microwave-safe mug lightly with nonstick spray. Add bread cubes, egg substitute, ham, and cheese wedge, breaking cheese into pieces as you add it. Mix gently. Microwave for 1 minute.

Lightly stir, and then top with shredded cheese. Microwave for another 45 to 60 seconds, until scramble is just set.

Stir and enjoy!

MAKES 1 SERVING

egg mug lorraine

Who is this Lorraine and how does she make her eggs taste so delicious?!

PER SERVING (entire mug): 128 calories, 4g fat, 730mg sodium, 3.5g carbs, 0g fiber, 2g sugars, 17.5g protein

○ Ingredients

½ cup fat-free liquid egg substitute
1 wedge The Laughing Cow Light Original Swiss cheese
1 tablespoon precooked real crumbled bacon
1 teaspoon dried minced onion
½ teaspoon Dijonnaise

○ Directions

Spray a large microwave-safe mug lightly with nonstick spray. Add all ingredients, breaking cheese wedge into pieces as you add it, and stir. Microwave for 1 minute.

Stir gently, and then microwave for another 45 to 60 seconds, until scramble is just set.

Stir and enjoy!

MAKES 1 SERVING

egg mug mexicali

Have trouble waking up in the AM? Try making this one with super-spicy salsa!

PER SERVING (entire mug): 116 calories, 0.5g fat, 579mg sodium, 5.5g carbs, 1.5g fiber, 1.5g sugars, 21.5g protein

○ Ingredients

½ cup fat-free liquid egg substitute
¼ cup frozen ground-beef-style soy crumbles
2 tablespoons shredded fat-free cheddar cheese
1 tablespoon salsa

○ Directions

Spray a large microwave-safe mug lightly with nonstick spray. Add egg substitute, soy crumbles, and cheese, and stir. Microwave for 1 minute.

Stir gently, and then microwave for another 45 to 60 seconds, until scramble is just set.

Stir, top with salsa, and enjoy!

MAKES 1 SERVING

For more recipes, tips & tricks, food finds, and MORE, sign up for FREE daily emails at hungry-girl.com!

sausage spaghetti swap

Capers, marinara, sausage . . . noodles?! This is a head-explodingly good Italian dish. Try it, and let's hope your head doesn't actually explode. Thanks for the inspiration, Anna!

PER SERVING (entire recipe): 285 calories, 12g fat, 1,250mg sodium, 20g carbs, 6g fiber, 10.5g sugars, 22g protein

o Ingredients

1 package House Foods Tofu Shirataki Spaghetti Shaped Noodle Substitute
1 precooked 3-ounce chicken or meatless sausage link with 8g fat or less, sliced
½ cup low-fat marinara sauce
½ tablespoon jarred capers, drained
2 teaspoons reduced-fat Parmesan-style grated topping
Salt, black pepper, garlic powder, and dried oregano, to taste

o Directions

Using a strainer, rinse and drain shirataki noodles well. Pat dry. In a microwave-safe bowl, microwave noodles for 1 minute. Drain excess liquid. Dry as thoroughly as possible, using paper towels. Cut noodles up a bit.

Add all other ingredients to the bowl and mix well. Microwave for 1 to 2 minutes, until heated. Enjoy!

MAKES 1 SERVING

HG Tip!

If using frozen sausage, do not thaw completely. This will make it easier to slice.

cheesy beefy supreme wrap

Don't let the name fool you. This one is completely meat-free. It's also cheesy, creamy, and amazingly delicious.

> **PER SERVING** (entire recipe): 262 calories, 4.25g fat, 1,178mg sodium, 31.5g carbs, 8g fiber, 2.5g sugars, 30g protein

o Ingredients

½ cup frozen ground-beef-style soy crumbles
½ wedge The Laughing Cow Light Original Swiss cheese
½ teaspoon dry taco seasoning mix
1 teaspoon taco sauce
1 burrito-size flour tortilla with about 110 calories
⅓ cup shredded fat-free cheddar cheese
1 tablespoon fat-free sour cream

o Directions

Place soy crumbles, cheese wedge half, and taco seasoning in a microwave-safe bowl, breaking cheese into pieces as you add it. Microwave for 1 minute. Add taco sauce and mix well. Set aside.

Lay tortilla flat on a microwave-safe plate, and warm it in the microwave for about 10 seconds. Place soy crumble mixture in the center of the tortilla and top with shredded cheese.

Return plate to the microwave, with the tortilla not yet folded, and cook for about 40 seconds, until shredded cheese begins to melt.

Top cheese with sour cream. Wrap the tortilla up by first folding in the sides and then rolling it up from the bottom.

With the seam-side down on the plate, heat in the microwave for 30 seconds. Enjoy!

MAKES 1 SERVING

italian-style bacon alfredo bowl

Thanks to Pam for inspiring this recipe. No one would EVER believe that this dish is so low in calories and fat grams. It's ridiculously decadent and slightly addictive. Luckily, we're pretty sure you can't OD on guilt-free bacon bowls . . .

PER SERVING (entire bowl): 266 calories, 7.5g fat, 951mg sodium, 15g carbs, 5.25g fiber, 4g sugars, 34g protein

○ Ingredients

1 package House Foods Tofu Shirataki Spaghetti Shaped Noodle Substitute

1 tablespoon fat-free sour cream

2 teaspoons reduced-fat Parmesan-style grated topping

1 wedge The Laughing Cow Light Original Swiss cheese

3 ounces cooked boneless skinless lean chicken breast, roughly chopped

¼ cup jarred roasted red peppers packed in water, drained and roughly chopped

¼ cup canned sliced mushrooms, drained

Salt and black pepper, to taste

1 tablespoon precooked real crumbled bacon

○ Directions

Use a strainer to rinse and drain shirataki noodles well. Pat dry. In a microwave-safe bowl, microwave for 1 minute. Drain excess liquid. Dry as thoroughly as possible, using paper towels. Cut noodles up a bit.

Top noodles with sour cream, grated topping, and cheese wedge, breaking cheese into pieces as you add it. Microwave for 1 minute. Mix thoroughly.

Add all other ingredients except bacon, salt, and black pepper to the bowl, and mix well. Microwave for 1 to 2 minutes, until heated.

Season to taste with salt and black pepper. Sprinkle with bacon and enjoy!

MAKES 1 SERVING

📷 For a pic of this recipe, see the first photo insert. Yay!

Extra, Extra!

Roasted red peppers need not go to waste . . . use 'em in a Veggie-Packed Wrap Attack (page 118) or some Slow-Cookin' Mexican Chicken (page 182)!

Extra, Extra!

Don't ditch the remaining canned mushrooms! Use 'em to make some Sloppy Joe-chiladas (page 84), Mom-Style Creamy Chicken 'n Veggies (page 146), or a Happy Camper Cheeseburger Crumble (page 156)!

blt pasta salad

This chilled noodle salad is a unique and crazy-delicious spin on the whole BLT thing. Special thanks to Meghan for inspiring it!

> **PER SERVING** (entire recipe): 155 calories, 7.5g fat, 585mg sodium, 14g carbs, 5g fiber, 2g sugars, 9.5g protein

Ingredients

1 package House Foods Tofu Shirataki Fettuccine Shaped Noodle Substitute
¼ cup torn lettuce leaves
2 tablespoons sun-dried tomatoes packed in oil, drained and roughly chopped
2 tablespoons precooked real crumbled bacon
1 tablespoon chopped scallions
1 tablespoon fat-free mayonnaise
1 tablespoon fat-free sour cream

Directions

Using a strainer, rinse and drain shirataki noodles well. Pat dry. In a microwave-safe bowl, microwave noodles for 1 minute. Drain excess liquid. Dry as thoroughly as possible, using paper towels. Cut noodles up a bit. Refrigerate for about 20 minutes, until completely chilled.

Add all other ingredients to the bowl and mix well. Enjoy!

MAKES 1 SERVING

buffalo vegetable hungry girlfredo

Holy hotness! This spicy yet creamy take on fettuccine Alfredo will blow you away. Thanks for the inspiration, Stacey!

> **PER SERVING** (entire recipe): 215 calories, 6g fat, 752mg sodium, 27g carbs, 8g fiber, 7g sugars, 11.5g protein

Ingredients

1 package House Foods Tofu Shirataki Fettuccine Shaped Noodle Substitute
2 teaspoons reduced-fat Parmesan-style grated topping
2 wedges The Laughing Cow Light Original Swiss cheese
1 cup frozen mixed vegetables
5 splashes Frank's RedHot Original Cayenne Pepper Sauce
Salt and black pepper, to taste

Directions

Using a strainer, rinse and drain shirataki noodles well. Pat dry. In a microwave-safe bowl, microwave noodles for 1 minute. Drain excess liquid. Dry as thoroughly as possible, using paper towels. Cut noodles up a bit.

Add grated topping and cheese wedges to the noodles, breaking wedges into pieces as you add them. Microwave for 1 minute, and then stir thoroughly. Set aside.

Microwave vegetables in a separate microwave-safe bowl until thawed and warm. Drain any excess liquid, and then add to noodles.

Add hot sauce and mix well. Microwave for 1 minute.

Season to taste with salt and pepper. Then enjoy!

MAKES 1 SERVING

83

sloppy joe-chiladas

Sloppy Joes are so good, why hold them back? We've let them branch out into the world of enchiladas. Who knows, Sloppy Joe nachos, Sloppy Joe chili, and Sloppy Joe hot dogs could be next . . .

> **PER SERVING** (2 enchiladas): 214 calories, 2.5g fat, 851mg sodium, 36.5g carbs, 7.25g fiber, 5g sugars, 14.5g protein

o Ingredients

¼ cup chopped onion
¼ cup chopped green bell pepper
1 cup frozen ground-beef-style soy crumbles
¼ cup canned sliced mushrooms, drained
1 teaspoon canned tomato paste

½ teaspoon dry taco seasoning mix
½ no-calorie sweetener packet
¾ cup canned tomato sauce
Four 6-inch corn tortillas

o Directions

Place onion and bell pepper in a microwave-safe bowl with 2 tablespoons water. Cover and microwave for 4 minutes. Once cool enough to handle, drain any excess water.

Add soy crumbles and mushrooms to the bowl. Microwave for 1 minute. Set aside.

In a separate microwave-safe bowl, mix tomato paste, taco seasoning, and sweetener into tomato sauce. Microwave for 30 seconds, or until thoroughly heated.

Reserve ¼ cup sauce to top the enchiladas, and add remaining sauce to the veggie-crumble mixture. Stir well, and set aside.

Dampen two paper towels and place the tortillas between them. Microwave for 1½ minutes.

Lay tortillas flat and evenly distribute the saucy veggie mixture between them.

Wrap each tortilla up tightly and place it on a microwave-safe plate with the seam-side down. Cover with the reserved sauce.

Microwave for about 20 seconds, until enchiladas are hot. Now enjoy!

MAKES 2 SERVINGS

 For a pic of this recipe, see the first photo insert. Yay!

Extra, Extra!

Use leftover mushrooms to make an Italian-Style Bacon Alfredo Bowl (page 80), some Mom-Style Creamy Chicken 'n Veggies (page 146), or a Happy Camper Cheeseburger Crumble (page 156)!

buff chick hot wing dip

This isn't just a dip for chips and veggies, humans. It's also been used as a sandwich spread, a shampoo, and even a salad dressing at the HG HQ. Okay, it's never been used as a shampoo. Just wanted to see if you were paying attention.

> **PER SERVING** (about ¼ cup): 68 calories, 1.5g fat, 616mg sodium, 2g carbs, 0g fiber, 1g sugars, 10g protein

o Ingredients

One 8-ounce tub fat-free cream cheese, room temperature
½ cup Frank's RedHot Original Cayenne Pepper Sauce
½ cup shredded part-skim mozzarella cheese
¼ cup fat-free ranch dressing
¼ cup fat-free plain Greek yogurt
Two 9.75-ounce (or 10-ounce) cans 98% fat-free chunk
        white chicken breast in water, drained and flaked

o Directions

Place cream cheese in a large microwave-safe bowl and stir until smooth. Mix in Frank's RedHot, mozzarella cheese, ranch dressing, and yogurt. Stir in chicken until thoroughly combined.

Microwave for 3 minutes. Stir and then microwave for an additional 2 minutes, or until hot. Enjoy!

MAKES 15 SERVINGS

 For a pic of this recipe, see the first photo insert. Yay!

cup o' chocolate-coconut bread pudding

Hot, sweet, chocolate–coconut–marshmallow fun in a cup. This weird and wonderful dessert will become one of your new BFFs!

PER SERVING (entire recipe): 215 calories, 2g fat, 755mg sodium, 33.5g carbs, 6g fiber, 11.5g sugars, 19g protein

Ingredients

One 25-calorie packet diet hot cocoa mix
Dash salt
½ cup fat-free liquid egg substitute
¼ teaspoon coconut extract
2 slices light white bread
1 teaspoon mini semi-sweet chocolate chips
10 mini marshmallows

Directions

Combine cocoa mix and salt in a glass. Add ¼ cup very hot water and stir until ingredients have dissolved. Add egg substitute and coconut extract, and stir. Set aside.

Toast bread and tear into cubes. Spray a large microwave-safe mug lightly with nonstick spray. Add bread cubes and top with cocoa-egg mixture. If needed, stir gently to ensure bread is thoroughly soaked. Top evenly with chocolate chips and marshmallows.

Microwave for about 2 minutes and 15 seconds, until bread pudding is set. (It will puff up once set.) Enjoy!

MAKES 1 SERVING

For a pic of this recipe, see the first photo insert. Yay!

cake on the beach

Creamy pudding . . . chilly pineapple topping . . . sweet yellow cake!?! It's like a little tropical vacation in a bowl!

> **PER SERVING** (1 cake with toppings): 136 calories, 2.5g fat, 217mg sodium, 27g carbs, <0.5g fiber, 14.5g sugars, 2g protein

o Ingredients

½ cup moist-style yellow cake mix
¼ cup fat-free vanilla yogurt
¼ cup canned crushed pineapple packed in juice, not drained
1 Jell-O Sugar Free Vanilla Pudding Snack
1 tablespoon shredded sweetened coconut

o Directions

Combine cake mix, yogurt, and 1 tablespoon water in a small bowl, and mix until smooth. Spray 3 small microwave-safe bowls with nonstick spray, and then evenly distribute cake mixture among them.

One at a time, microwave each bowl for about 45 seconds, until cake has risen and is puffy. Allow to cool for 5 minutes.

Using a toothpick, pierce holes into each mini cake. Spread cakes evenly first with pineapple and then with the pudding. Refrigerate for 1 hour, or until thoroughly chilled.

Sprinkle each cake with 1 teaspoon coconut and enjoy!

MAKES 3 SERVINGS

Extra, Extra!

Pineapple doesn't like to be wasted. Get blendy with our Slush-Puppy Pineapple Lemonade (page 194) or stir-crazy with Teriyaki Shrimp 'n Slaw Stir-Fry (page 268)!

expresso cake in a mug

Nope, that's not a typo. This is super-fast espresso cake, for true coffee lovers ONLY. (It's got a real java kick!)

> **PER SERVING** (entire recipe): 147 calories, 3.25g fat, 446mg sodium, 25.5g carbs, 0.5g fiber, 14.5g sugars, 3.5g protein

o Ingredients

1 teaspoon instant coffee granules
1 teaspoon mini semi-sweet
   chocolate chips
3 tablespoons devil's food cake mix
1 tablespoon fat-free sour cream

1 tablespoon fat-free liquid egg substitute
¼ teaspoon vanilla extract
⅛ teaspoon baking powder
1 no-calorie sweetener packet
Dash salt

o Directions

Place coffee granules and chocolate chips in a microwave-safe mug sprayed with nonstick spray. Add 2 tablespoons hot water and stir until ingredients have dissolved.

Add remaining ingredients and mix well. Microwave for 1 minute and 45 seconds.

Allow to cool slightly, and then enjoy!

MAKES 1 SERVING

For a pic of this recipe, see the first photo insert. Yay!

chapter four | Four Ingredients or Less

Each and every recipe on the following pages (a.k.a. Chapter 4) uses no more than FOUR ingredients.

But if you didn't already figure that out from the title, you probably shouldn't be trusted around sharp kitchen utensils and/or open flames. Just sayin' . . .

the american classic pita

It's bacon, egg, and cheese in a pita. Like the name says . . . CLASSIC.

> **PER SERVING** (entire recipe): 307 calories, 6g fat,
> 1,215mg sodium, 31g carbs, 5.5g fiber, 3g sugars, 32g protein

o Ingredients

2 slices center-cut bacon or turkey bacon
⅔ cup fat-free liquid egg substitute
1 slice fat-free cheddar cheese, torn into pieces
1 whole-wheat or high-fiber pita

o Directions

Prepare bacon according to package directions, either in the microwave or in a skillet sprayed with nonstick spray. Set aside.

Bring a skillet sprayed with nonstick spray to medium heat. Add egg substitute and scramble for 2 to 3 minutes, until fully cooked.

Top scramble evenly with cheese pieces and remove from heat. Chop or crumble bacon, and sprinkle over the scramble. Gently mix with a spatula.

Warm pita in the microwave for 10 to 15 seconds. Slice it in half, and stuff your cheesy bacon 'n eggs into the two pockets. Happy chewing!

MAKES 1 SERVING

grillin' of the corn

Sweet, grilled, and garlicky. Just the way corn oughta be!

PER SERVING (entire cob): 128 calories, 1.25g fat, 900mg sodium, 28g carbs, 2.5g fiber, 10.5g sugars, 3g protein

o Ingredients

2 tablespoons thick teriyaki sauce with 20 to 25 calories per tablespoon
½ teaspoon crushed garlic
1 fresh cob of corn, husk removed

o Directions

In a small bowl, mix teriyaki sauce and garlic.

Place corn on the cob in the center of a large piece of foil. Spread garlic-teriyaki sauce across the corn, turning the cob so the marinade is evenly distributed. Wrap cob up securely in the foil, making sure there is no place for the marinade to escape.

Bring grill to medium-high heat. With the grill cover down, grill foil-wrapped corn for about 15 minutes, carefully turning occasionally with long barbecue tongs.

Remove from grill and allow to cool slightly. Once cool enough to handle, remove foil and eat!

MAKES 1 SERVING

You'll Need: large sealable plastic bag, meat mallet or a heavy can, toothpicks, baking pan, nonstick spray, aluminum foil

Prep: 10 minutes   Cook: 35 minutes

stuffed chick cordon bleu

Make this super-simple chicken dish for guests, and everyone will think you worked for HOURS in your kitchen.

> **PER SERVING** (entire recipe): 222 calories, 4.5g fat, 692mg sodium, 2g carbs, 0g fiber, 1g sugars, 40g protein

o Ingredients

One 5-ounce raw boneless skinless lean chicken breast cutlet
Salt and black pepper, to taste
1 wedge The Laughing Cow Light Original Swiss cheese
1 ounce (about 2 slices) 97 to 98% fat-free ham

o Directions

Preheat oven to 350 degrees.

Place chicken in a large sealable plastic bag, squeeze out as much air as you can, and seal. Using a meat mallet or a heavy can, carefully pound chicken until it is about ¼-inch thick. Remove chicken from the bag, and season to taste with salt and pepper on both sides.

Lay the chicken flat and spread the cheese wedge over it. Evenly layer the ham slices on top of the cheese. Starting with one of the longer sides (or any side, if it's square), tightly roll up the chicken breast cutlet, and secure with toothpicks.

Place chicken roll in a baking pan sprayed with nonstick spray, and then cover the pan with foil. Bake in the oven for 20 minutes.

Carefully remove the foil. Continue to bake, uncovered, for an additional 15 minutes, or until chicken is cooked through.

Remove toothpicks and enjoy!

MAKES 1 SERVING

 For a pic of this recipe, see the first photo insert. Yay!

backyard bbq beef cups

There are no words to describe the awesomeness of these things. But here goes an attempt: tasty, sweet, yummy, puffy, delicious, awesome, dreamy, and party-tastic.

> **PER SERVING** (1 "beef cup"): 125 calories, 4g fat, 321mg sodium, 15g carbs, <0.5g fiber, 7g sugars, 7g protein

o Ingredients

12 ounces raw extra-lean ground beef
1 small onion, finely chopped
¾ cup barbecue sauce
1 package Pillsbury Crescent Recipe Creations Seamless Dough Sheet

o Directions

Preheat oven to 375 degrees. Spray a 12-cup muffin pan with nonstick spray and set aside.

Bring a large skillet sprayed with nonstick spray to medium-high heat. Add beef and onion. Stirring frequently, cook until beef is crumbled and browned and onion is soft, about 8 to 10 minutes.

Reduce heat to low. Stir in BBQ sauce and let simmer for 5 minutes.

Roll dough out into a 12-inch by 9-inch rectangle. Using a knife or pizza cutter, cut into 12 squares.

Place each square into a muffin cup, and press it into the bottom and up along the sides to form a little "dough cup" for the beef.

Evenly distribute beef mixture among the cups. Bake in the oven for 12 to 15 minutes, until golden brown.

Let cool slightly, and then chow down!

MAKES 12 SERVINGS

For a pic of this recipe, see the first photo insert. Yay!

HG Alternative!

These can also be made with lean ground turkey, ground-beef-style soy crumbles, or shredded chicken.

For Weight Watchers **POINTS**® values and photos of all the recipes in this book, check out hungry-girl.com/book.

too-ez mac 'n cheese

Mac 'n cheese may actually be the most requested HG recipe ever. This version is so creamy and cheesy. Thanks to the help of cauliflower, which tastes SO good with whole-wheat pasta and cheese, the portion size is pretty huge for the calorie count. AMAZING!

> **PER SERVING** (¼th of recipe, about 1 cup): 202 calories, 4.5g fat, 825mg sodium, 36g carbs, 5g fiber, 6g sugars, 8.5g protein

o Ingredients

2 cups uncooked whole-wheat-blend rotini pasta
6 cups (about 24 ounces) frozen Green Giant Cauliflower & Cheese Sauce
3 wedges The Laughing Cow Light Original Swiss cheese
Optional: salt and black pepper

o Directions

In a large pot, prepare pasta according to the instructions on the package; drain well and set aside. While pasta is cooking, place contents of the cauliflower & sauce package in a large microwave-safe bowl. Cover and microwave for 10 to 12 minutes, until sauce has melted and cauliflower is hot.

Once the bowl is cool enough to handle, remove it from the microwave and add cooked pasta. Set aside.

Unwrap cheese wedges and place in a small microwave-safe bowl. Microwave for 30 seconds. Stir until smooth, and then add to the large bowl with the pasta.

Mix thoroughly, ensuring that the Laughing Cow cheese is evenly distributed and the pasta and cauliflower are coated in cheese sauce. If you like, season to taste with salt and pepper. Enjoy!

MAKES 4 SERVINGS

 For a pic of this recipe, see the first photo insert. Yay!

shrimp cocktail tacos

We took a classic seafood appetizer and turned it into a delicious meal. These chilly tacos ROCK!

> **PER SERVING** (2 tacos, entire recipe): 243 calories, 5g fat, 638mg sodium, 26.5g carbs, 3.5g fiber, 4g sugars, 21g protein

o Ingredients

3 ounces cooked ready-to-eat shrimp, chopped
¼ cup plus 2 tablespoons black bean and corn salsa
2 corn taco shells
¼ cup shredded lettuce

o Directions

Mix shrimp and salsa in a bowl, cover, and refrigerate for at least 30 minutes.

Evenly distribute lettuce between taco shells, and top with shrimp-salsa mixture. Now chomp!

MAKES 1 SERVING

 For a pic of this recipe, see the first photo insert. Yay!

cheesy crab 'n chile quesadilla

WOW, this thing is good. Those green chiles are AWESOME with crab and cheese. Feel free to cheat the whole four-ingredients thing and serve this quesadilla with salsa and fat-free sour cream. I won't tell . . .

> **PER SERVING** (entire quesadilla): 193 calories, 4.5g fat, 1,080mg sodium, 26.5g carbs, 6g fiber, 3.5g sugars, 17.5g protein

o Ingredients

Half a 6-ounce can (about ½ cup) crabmeat, drained and flaked
1 wedge The Laughing Cow Light Original Swiss cheese
3 tablespoons canned diced green chiles
1 burrito-size flour tortilla with about 110 calories

o Directions

Combine crabmeat, cheese, and chiles in a bowl, and mix thoroughly.

Bring a skillet sprayed with nonstick spray to medium heat. Place tortilla flat in the skillet and spread crab mixture over one half of the tortilla. Fold the other half of the tortilla over to form the quesadilla, and then press down firmly with a spatula to seal.

Cook until both sides are crispy, about 2 minutes per side. Remove from heat and cut into triangles. Enjoy!

MAKES 1 SERVING

Extra, Extra!

Have an open can of chiles? Whip up a **Bursting Burrito Bowl** (page 136), **Chunky Veggie Pumpkin Chili** (page 176), or **Slow-Cookin' Mexican Chicken** (page 182)!

creamed corn-cheese bites

Holy moly! These adorable little corn-packed puffs are indescribably AMAZING. So I'm not even going to attempt to describe them.

> **PER SERVING** (1 "cheese bite"): 46 calories, 2g fat, 122mg sodium, 6g carbs, <0.5g fiber, 1g sugars, 1g protein

○ Ingredients

1 tablespoon flour
½ package Pillsbury Crescent Recipe Creations Seamless Dough Sheet
½ cup canned cream-style corn
¼ cup shredded reduced-fat cheddar cheese

○ Directions

Preheat oven to 350 degrees.

Prepare a dry surface by dusting it with some of the flour. Dust a rolling pin with the flour, as well.

Roll dough out into a 12-inch by 9-inch rectangle. Using a knife or pizza cutter, cut dough into 12 squares. Gently press each square into a mini muffin cup, leaving corners of dough extended over edge of each cup.

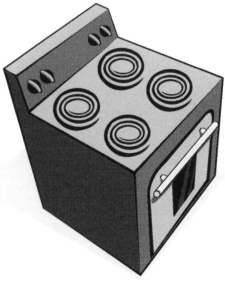

Spoon cream-style corn evenly into dough-lined cups. Top each with cheese. Fold the dough edges down, so they cover the top.

Bake in the oven for 10 to 12 minutes, until edges are golden brown and filling is set.

Let stand for 5 minutes. Enjoy!

MAKES 12 SERVINGS

Extra, Extra!

It's best to use the refrigerated dough soon after you open it. So make a second batch of this recipe ASAP, or make some Jammin' Tarts (page 260)!

For more recipes, tips & tricks, food finds, and MORE, sign up for FREE daily emails at hungry-girl.com!

quickie caramel custard

This simple snack/dessert is yummy and crazy-high in protein, thanks to the goodness of Greek yogurt.

PER SERVING (entire recipe): 97 calories, 0g fat, 66mg sodium, 8.5g carbs, <0.5g fiber, 6.5g sugars, 15g protein

o Ingredients

¾ cup fat-free plain Greek yogurt
1 tablespoon Splenda No Calorie Sweetener (granulated)
1½ teaspoons sugar-free calorie-free caramel syrup
¼ teaspoon cinnamon

o Directions

Mix ingredients together in a bowl and serve with your favorite spoon!

MAKES 1 SERVING

HG Tip!

Torani makes the best sugar-free, calorie-free syrup out there. Visit the company's website to see where the syrups are sold near you or to order online!

Can't find syrup at the store (or don't feel like purchasing an entire bottle)? Just stop by Starbucks and order a shot of sugar-free caramel syrup to go.

bffs (black forest fillo-cups)

Here's some chocolate–cherry–whipped–cream madness for ya! Mmmmmmm . . .

> **PER SERVING** (3 "fillo-cups"): 80 calories, 3.5g fat, 70mg sodium, 12.5g carbs, 0.5g fiber, 3g sugars, 0.5g protein

○ Ingredients

15 frozen Athens Mini Fillo Shells (1 box)
1 Jell-O Sugar Free Double Chocolate Pudding Snack
15 teaspoons Fat Free Reddi-wip
15 pitted dark sweet cherries, fresh or thawed from frozen

○ Directions

Preheat oven to 350 degrees.

Place shells on a baking sheet sprayed lightly with nonstick spray. Bake in the oven for 3 to 5 minutes, until golden and crispy. Allow to cool for several minutes.

Evenly distribute pudding among shells, and top each with a 1-teaspoon squirt of Reddi-wip. Add a cherry to each cup, and prepare for some quality time with your new BFFs!

MAKES 5 SERVINGS

 For a pic of this recipe, see the first photo insert. Yay!

HG Tip!

Pssst . . . See the "Couples" section for more fillo shell ideas ASAP!

chapter five | Cook-Me-Not

There's no need to cook the recipes here,

and therefore this chapter is very appropriately named.
Have fun assembling, humans!

ginormous sweet-tart fruit salad

A big fat thank-you to HG pal Debbie for inspiring this super-sized fruit salad!

> **PER SERVING** (1⅓ cups): 100 calories, 0.5g fat, 71mg sodium, 23.5g carbs, 2.5g fiber, 17g sugars, 1.5g protein

○ Ingredients

3 tablespoons freshly squeezed orange juice
1 tablespoon finely chopped fresh mint
2 teaspoons seasoned rice vinegar
1 teaspoon granulated sugar
1⅔ cups peeled and diced cucumber

1 cup chopped red grapefruit segments
(if packaged, packed in juice
and drained)
¾ cup diced strawberries
¾ cup blueberries

○ Directions

In a small bowl, combine orange juice, mint, vinegar, and sugar. Stir until blended. Set aside.

Place all other ingredients in a large bowl. Pour orange juice mixture over the contents and stir gently to coat.

Cover and refrigerate for at least 1 hour (overnight is best). Stir gently just before serving. Enjoy!!!

MAKES 3 SERVINGS

salmon spread the love

It's a spread that's also a dip that's also DELICIOUS. No one would ever guess it's made with canned salmon—it tastes just like a fancy deli spread. Enjoy it on English muffins, tortillas, cut-up veggies, and SO much more . . .

PER SERVING (about ¼ cup): 78 calories, 1.75g fat, 464mg sodium, 3g carbs, 0g fiber, 1.5g sugars, 11.5g protein

o Ingredients

One 8-ounce tub fat-free cream cheese, room temperature
2 wedges The Laughing Cow Light Original Swiss cheese
1½ tablespoons Dijonnaise
½ teaspoon lemon juice
One 5-ounce can skinless boneless pink salmon in water, drained and finely flaked
1 tablespoon dried minced onion

o Directions

In a medium bowl, combine cream cheese, cheese wedges, Dijonnaise, and lemon juice. Mix thoroughly, until ingredients are completely integrated.

Add salmon and onion and stir thoroughly, until a very smooth consistency is reached.

Cover and refrigerate for at least 1 hour. (It tastes sooo good the next day!)

MAKES 6 SERVINGS

crab-happy sunomono salad

I LOVE sunomono salad (typically it's just thinly sliced cucumber in rice vinegar). This HG version is DELICIOUS: sweet, tangy, crunchy, and crab-loaded. It's a great starter, snack, or mini-meal. Keep a tub of it in the fridge, and munch on it when hunger attacks!

> **PER SERVING** (1 heaping cup): 95 calories, 0.5g fat, 575mg sodium, 16g carbs, 1g fiber, 5g sugars, 6.5g protein

○ Ingredients

5 small Persian cucumbers (or any small, thin-skinned cucumbers)

1 red bell pepper

12 ounces (about 2 cups) chunk-style imitation crab

¼ cup seasoned rice vinegar

1 teaspoon lime juice

1 teaspoon reduced-sodium/lite soy sauce

2 no-calorie sweetener packets

○ Directions

Cut off cucumber ends and very thinly slice cucumbers into rounds. Very thinly slice bell pepper into strips about 2 inches long. Transfer veggies to a large bowl and set aside.

If needed, chop crab into bite-sized pieces. Add those to the bowl with the veggies, toss to mix, and set aside.

In a separate bowl, combine vinegar, lime juice, soy sauce, and sweetener. Add ½ cup cold water and mix well. Pour mixture over the veggies and crab and gently stir.

Cover and chill in the fridge for at least 3 hours (overnight is best). Then stir and enjoy!

MAKES 6 SERVINGS

twice-tomatoed turkey tortilla

Yup, this wrap has TWO kinds of tomatoes. And turkey. And cheese. And it is DELICIOUS. This tomato-centric turkey treat is a real tongue-pleaser (and tongue-twister!).

> **PER SERVING** (entire wrap): 277 calories, 7.5g fat, 670mg sodium, 30g carbs, 8g fiber, 3.5g sugars, 27g protein

○ Ingredients

1 wedge The Laughing Cow Light Original Swiss cheese
3 tablespoons sun-dried tomatoes packed in oil, drained and chopped
1 burrito-size flour tortilla with about 110 calories
3 slices tomato
2 ounces cooked boneless skinless lean turkey breast, sliced
1 cup chopped romaine lettuce
Optional: Dijonnaise

○ Directions

In a small bowl, mix cheese with sun-dried tomatoes. Lay tortilla flat and spread with cheese-tomato mixture.

Place tomato slices and turkey slices along the center of the tortilla. If you like, top with Dijonnaise (we highly recommend it!).

Place lettuce in the center of the tortilla. Fold in the sides of the tortilla, and then carefully roll tortilla up from bottom to top. Enjoy!

MAKES 1 SERVING

HG Tip!

In a pinch, you can use prepackaged 98% fat-free turkey slices. Just know that those contain quite a lot of sodium.

slammin' slaw

Classic slaw, without all the classic calories and fat grams. Good riddance.

> **PER SERVING** (⅔ cup): 49 calories, <0.5g fat, 304mg sodium, 9.5g carbs, 2g fiber, 5g sugars, 1g protein

○ Ingredients

One 16-ounce bag dry cole slaw
¼ cup fat-free mayonnaise
¼ cup fat-free sour cream
2½ tablespoons seasoned rice vinegar

1 teaspoon Dijonnaise
2 no-calorie sweetener packets
¼ teaspoon seasoned salt
Salt and black pepper, to taste

○ Directions

Place cole slaw in a large bowl. Set aside.

To make dressing, in a small bowl, combine mayo, sour cream, rice vinegar, Dijonnaise, sweetener, and seasoned salt. Mix well.

Add dressing to cole slaw and stir until slaw is thoroughly coated.

Cover and refrigerate for at least 3 hours. (For best flavor, make slaw the night before you plan to serve it.)

Give it a good stir before serving, and season to taste with salt and pepper. Enjoy!

MAKES 6 SERVINGS

shrimped-up sweet corn 'n tomato salad

You need to do a whole lotta choppin' to prep this no-cook dish. But it is SO worth it! It's light, refreshing, and a great side salad or mini-meal option.

> **PER SERVING** (1 cup): 95 calories, 1g fat, 472mg sodium, 13g carbs, 2.5g fiber, 6g sugars, 9g protein

o Ingredients

6 ounces cooked ready-to-eat
    shrimp, chopped
2 cups diced plum tomatoes (about
    4 tomatoes' worth)
1 cup chopped red onion
1 cup canned sweet corn kernels, drained

½ cup diced seedless (or deseeded)
    cucumber
½ cup chopped cilantro
¾ teaspoon coarse salt
1 lemon
1 lime

o Directions

In a large bowl, mix all ingredients except lemon and lime.

Over a strainer, squeeze juice from the lemon and lime into the bowl, and then toss to coat.

Set in the fridge for at least 1 hour, to allow flavors to combine. NOW CHEW!!!

MAKES 5 SERVINGS

Extra, Extra!

Open can of corn, meet Chicken-with-a-Kick Pack (page 148)!

gazpacho surprise

Surprise! This chilly tomato-based soup's made with FRUIT. There, the secret's out. Now the only surprise left is how AMAZING it tastes.

PER SERVING (1 generous cup): 106 calories, 0.5g fat, 527mg sodium, 24g carbs, 4.5g fiber, 15.5g sugars, 3g protein

Ingredients

One 28-ounce can crushed tomatoes
2 cups V8 100% Vegetable Juice
1 cucumber, finely chopped
1 small red onion, finely chopped
1 Fuji apple, cored and finely chopped
1 cup blueberries
2 tablespoons chopped fresh basil

2 tablespoons balsamic vinegar
1 teaspoon chopped garlic
1 no-calorie sweetener packet
¼ teaspoon salt, or more to taste
⅛ teaspoon black pepper, or more to taste
1 lime

Directions

Combine all ingredients except lime in a large bowl. Using a strainer to catch any seeds, squeeze the juice from the lime into the bowl. Stir well.

Transfer half of the mixture to a blender, and puree until smooth. Return mixture to the bowl and mix well.

Cover and refrigerate for at least 2 hours.

If you like, season to taste with additional salt and pepper. Enjoy!

MAKES 6 SERVINGS

HG Tip!

This stuff doubles
as an awesome
fruity salsa!

For Weight Watchers *POINTS*®
values and photos of all the
recipes in this book, check out
hungry-girl.com/book.

veggie-packed wrap attack

This super-simple, herbed-up roll-up will be a new staple in your veggie-loving home.

> **PER SERVING** (entire wrap): 214 calories, 8g fat, 521mg sodium, 31g carbs, 10g fiber, 4.5g sugars, 11.5g protein

o Ingredients

1½ tablespoons fat-free cream cheese, room temperature
½ tablespoon chopped fresh basil
⅛ teaspoon dried oregano
1 burrito-size flour tortilla with about 110 calories

½ cup fresh spinach
¼ cup chopped cucumber
¼ cup chopped tomato
2 tablespoons jarred roasted red peppers packed in water, drained and chopped
¼ cup sliced avocado

o Directions

In a small dish, mix cream cheese with basil and oregano.

Lay tortilla flat and spread with cream cheese mixture. Pile on the spinach, cucumber, tomato, red peppers, and avocado. Wrap tortilla up by folding in the sides first, and then rolling it up tightly from the bottom.

Enjoy!

MAKES 1 SERVING

Extra, Extra!

Got an open jar of roasted red peppers? Sounds like a good time to make an Italian-Style Bacon Alfredo Bowl (page 80) or Slow-Cookin' Mexican Chicken (page 182)!

double-o-cinnamon apple breakfast bowl

Who knew cinnamon and apples and cottage cheese could have so much delicious, crazy fun together?! This is a fantastic and easy breakfast, but it can also be a light lunch or a sweet, refreshing snack. So many options . . . and SO much delicious cinnamon!!!

> **PER SERVING** (entire bowl): 182 calories, 0.5g fat, 429mg sodium, 32.5g carbs, 5g fiber, 24g sugars, 13.5g protein

o Ingredients

½ cup fat-free cottage cheese
1 no-calorie sweetener packet
1 drop vanilla extract
½ teaspoon cinnamon, divided
1 Fuji apple, cored and cubed

o Directions

Place cottage cheese in a bowl with sweetener, vanilla extract, and ¼ teaspoon cinnamon. Mix well.

Top with apple cubes, and then sprinkle with remaining ¼ teaspoon cinnamon. Enjoy!

MAKES 1 SERVING

chapter six | Fast Food Faves . . . Fast!

Fast food is kinda scary but kinda delicious, too.

(Just being honest here.) Instead of waiting in line at the drive-thru for potentially horrific food items, whip up these speedy, better-for-you versions in your kitchen. You'll save time, money, and ridiculous amounts of calories and fat grams.

big bowl of breakfast

This is a super-fun recipe that'll make you feel like you're eating a ginormous and delicious egg-y drive-thru breakfast. The difference is that yours will have a tiny fraction of the fat and calories. Go, you!

> **PER SERVING** (entire recipe): 262 calories, 3.5g fat, 1,306mg sodium, 23.5g carbs, 5g fiber, 4g sugars, 31g protein

o Ingredients

1 tray frozen Green Giant Just for One Broccoli & Cheese Sauce
¾ cup fat-free liquid egg substitute
¾ cup frozen potatoes O'Brien
1 slice Canadian bacon, chopped
2 tablespoons shredded fat-free cheddar cheese

o Directions

Prepare broccoli & cheese sauce according to package instructions. Set aside.

Bring a large skillet sprayed with nonstick spray to medium heat. Add egg substitute and scramble for 2 to 3 minutes, until fully cooked. Place scrambled egg substitute in a microwave-safe bowl and set aside.

Remove skillet from heat, re-spray with nonstick spray, and return to the stove. Raise heat to medium-high and add potatoes. Cook for 3 to 4 minutes, stirring occasionally, until thawed and lightly browned.

Add Canadian bacon and cook until hot and a little crispy, about 1 to 2 minutes.

Add potato-bacon mixture to the bowl with the egg scramble. Add broccoli & cheese sauce and mix to combine.

Sprinkle shredded cheese on top of the bowl, and microwave for 30 to 45 seconds, until cheese has melted. Grab a sturdy fork and dig in!

MAKES 1 SERVING

For a pic of this recipe, see the first photo insert. Yay!

Extra, Extra!

Have an open bag of potatoes O'Brien? Whip up a College Breakfast Burrito (page 70) or a Happy Camper Cheeseburger Crumble (page 156)!

no-buns-about-it
animal-style cheeseburger

In-N-Out Burger is one of my OBSESSIONS, and it's totally possible to eat there guilt-free—a single Protein Style burger with ketchup and mustard (instead of the special sauce) has just 160 calories. But not everyone has an In-N-Out where they live, and even if they do, the lines are CRAZY. Now you can enjoy the same AMAZING burger-ific taste at home. I've stepped it up by doing a swap for the fatty 'n famous "animal-style" burger. Yum!

> **PER SERVING** (entire recipe): 162 calories, 1g fat, 1,000mg sodium, 23g carbs, 6g fiber, 9g sugars, 19g protein

Ingredients

1 extra-large leaf iceberg or butter lettuce
3 hamburger dill pickle chips
1 Boca Original Meatless Burger (Vegan)
1 teaspoon yellow mustard
1 slice fat-free cheddar cheese
⅓ cup chopped onion
1½ tablespoons fat-free thousand island dressing

Directions

Lay lettuce on a plate and place pickle chips in the center. Set aside.

Bring a skillet sprayed with nonstick spray to medium-high heat. Place Boca burger in the skillet, cook for 2 minutes, and then flip the burger.

Spread mustard on the burger, still in the skillet, and cook for an additional 1 to 2 minutes, until burger is cooked through.

Top burger with cheese and continue cooking until cheese begins to melt. Place burger over the pickles on the lettuce and set aside.

Remove skillet from heat, re-spray with nonstick spray, and return to medium-high heat. Add onion and cook until soft, about 3 minutes.

Place onion over the burger and top with dressing. Wrap lettuce up and around your burger and begin chewing!

MAKES 1 SERVING

sweet 'n sassy boneless hot wings

Yup, they're sweet and TOTALLY sassy. These are addictively delicious and will become a new staple in your home (if you're smart!).

PER SERVING (entire recipe): 267 calories, 1.5g fat, 775mg sodium, 30g carbs, 2g fiber, 15g sugars, 31g protein

○ Ingredients

4 ounces raw boneless skinless lean
    chicken breast, cut into 8 nuggets
2 tablespoons fat-free liquid egg substitute
2 tablespoons whole-wheat flour
Dash salt

Dash black pepper
2 tablespoons sweet Asian chili sauce
1 teaspoon seasoned rice vinegar
¼ teaspoon crushed red pepper

○ Directions

Preheat oven to 375 degrees. Spray a baking sheet with nonstick spray and set aside.

Place chicken in a bowl, cover with egg substitute, and toss to coat. Set aside.

In a separate bowl, combine flour, salt, and black pepper, and mix well. One at a time, transfer chicken nuggets to the flour bowl, giving them a shake first to remove excess egg substitute—coat completely with flour, and then transfer to the baking sheet.

Bake in oven for about 16 minutes, flipping halfway through, until chicken is fully cooked. Remove from the oven and set aside.

Combine chili sauce, vinegar, and crushed red pepper in a bowl and mix well. Add chicken and toss to coat. Now gobble up!

MAKES 1 SERVING

 For a pic of this recipe, see the first photo insert. Yay!

Extra, Extra!

Sweet Asian chili sauce = awesome in Crazy Pineapple Salmon Teriyaki (page 154) and Sweet-Hot Steak Bites (page 188)!

chili-rific cheeseburger

Everyone craves a chili-burger now and then. (They do, don't they? Please tell me I'm normal!) A classic chili-burger has around 800 calories and a crazy-high fat count. Here's a fun little swap you can make at home that'll save you TONS in the calorie and fat departments. And it tastes JUST like a regular chili-burger. Pinky swear!

> **PER SERVING** (entire recipe): 230 calories, 2g fat, 1,330mg sodium, 35.5g carbs, 8g fiber, 6g sugars, 25g protein

Ingredients

1 small light hamburger bun (about 80 calories)
4 hamburger dill pickle chips
2 slices tomato
1 slice onion

1 Boca Original Meatless Burger (Vegan)
2 tablespoons low-fat veggie chili
1 slice fat-free American cheese
1 tablespoon yellow mustard

Directions

Split bun in half and toast lightly. Layer pickles, tomato, and onion on the bottom half of the bun.

Cook Boca patty according to the instructions on the box, either in a skillet with nonstick spray or in the microwave. Place burger over the veggies on the bun's bottom half.

HG Heads Up!
Sodium-counters can save about 450mg by nixing the pickles and mustard.

In a small microwave-safe bowl, microwave chili until hot.

Top the burger with the chili followed by the cheese slice. Slap the mustard onto the top half of the bun. Plop the bun top over the cheese and chili patty. Now, the most important step of all . . .

Enjoy!

MAKES 1 SERVING

HG Alternative!

Can't find 80-calorie buns? No worries! Get the lowest-calorie ones you can find, and adjust the nutritionals for this recipe accordingly.

For more recipes, tips & tricks, food finds, and MORE, sign up for FREE daily emails at hungry-girl.com!

island insanity burger

This is a take on an INSANELY fattening burger that's served at Red Robin. The version there has over a thousand calories! Ours is a total calorie-bargain. It's sweet, cheesy, and DEE-LICIOUS!

> **PER SERVING** (entire recipe): 239 calories, 1.5g fat, 1,250mg sodium, 41g carbs, 6g fiber, 14.5g sugars, 22.5g protein

○ Ingredients

1 pineapple ring packed in juice

1 Boca Original Meatless Burger (Vegan)

1 tablespoon thick teriyaki sauce with 20 to 25 calories per tablespoon, divided

1 slice fat-free cheddar cheese

1 small light hamburger bun (about 80 calories)

1 thick slice tomato

1 leaf lettuce

1 teaspoon fat-free mayonnaise

○ Directions

Bring a skillet sprayed with nonstick spray to medium-high heat. (If you have a grill pan, use it—you'll get neato grill marks.) Lay pineapple ring in the skillet/grill pan, and cook until slightly blackened and caramelized, about 3 minutes per side. Set aside to cool.

Cut a slit in the burger pouch. Place burger, slit-side up, in the microwave. Microwave for just about 1 minute, until warm. Remove patty from the pouch and place on a

Extra, Extra!

Canned pineapple has many uses. Like in our Pizza Luau (page 10) and Crazy Pineapple Salmon Teriyaki (page 154)!

microwave-safe plate. Pour half of the teriyaki sauce on top, spread it around, and flip patty to coat evenly on both sides. Lay cheese slice on top of the patty, and microwave for 30 additional seconds.

Place the burger patty on the bottom half of the bun, and top with the remaining teriyaki sauce. Add the pineapple ring, tomato, and lettuce. Spread mayo on the top half of the bun, and finish your burger off with the bun's top half. Now CHOMP!

MAKES 1 SERVING

HG Alternative!

Can't find 80-calorie buns? No worries! Get the lowest-calorie ones you can find, and adjust the nutritionals for this recipe accordingly.

blue-ribbon roast beef sandwich

Arby's, eat your heart out. This sandwich rocks. Jealous much?

> **PER SERVING** (entire recipe): 289 calories, 8.5g fat, 1,165mg sodium, 28g carbs, 6.75g fiber, 3g sugars, 27.5g protein

o Ingredients

1 light English muffin, split into halves
1 tablespoon light blue cheese dressing
    with about 25 calories per tablespoon
½ cup shredded lettuce
2 slices tomato

2 slices red onion
1 slice center-cut bacon or turkey bacon
⅛ teaspoon black pepper
3 ounces thinly sliced roast beef

o Directions

Bring a skillet sprayed with nonstick spray to medium heat. Lay muffin halves in the skillet with the insides facing down. Carefully remove once toasty, about 1 to 2 minutes.

Plate the muffin halves and evenly spread with dressing. Top the bottom half with lettuce, tomato, and onion. Set aside.

Remove skillet from the stove and re-spray with nonstick spray. Return skillet to the stove and bring to medium-high heat. Cut bacon in half widthwise, sprinkle with pepper, and lay it flat in the skillet. Cook until crispy, about 2 minutes on each side. Remove bacon and set aside.

Place roast beef in the skillet and, stirring occasionally, cook until warm and browned, about 1½ minutes.

Roughly chop the roast beef, if you like, or simply leave the slices whole. Place roast beef over the veggies on the bottom half of the muffin. Add bacon and finish it off with the top half of the muffin. Chow down!

MAKES 1 SERVING

For Weight Watchers *POINTS*®
values and photos of all the
recipes in this book, check out
hungry-girl.com/book.

queen-of-the-castle sliders

Sliders are the trendiest of all burgers. But trend or no trend, they're tasty and easy to HG–ize. Seeeeee?

PER SERVING (entire recipe, 4 sliders): 254 calories, 5.5g fat, 924mg sodium, 26g carbs, 6g fiber, 5.5g sugars, 29g protein

o Ingredients

4 ounces raw extra-lean ground beef

⅛ teaspoon salt

⅛ teaspoon onion powder

⅛ teaspoon garlic powder

⅛ teaspoon black pepper

⅓ cup chopped onion

2 slices light bread

4 hamburger dill pickle chips

Optional: ketchup, mustard

o Directions

Combine beef and seasonings in a small bowl, and knead mixture by hand until integrated. Divide seasoned beef evenly into four balls. Flatten and form each ball into a square patty on a plate. Using a knife, make four small slits on the top of each patty. Place in the freezer for 5 minutes.

Bring a skillet sprayed with nonstick spray to medium-high heat. Spread onion out in the skillet. Place the patties on top of the onion, slit-side down, and cover the skillet. Cook for 3 to 4 minutes (no flipping necessary), or until cooked through.

Meanwhile, cut each slice of bread into four squares, for a total of eight pieces. (If you like, slightly toast bread first.) Feel free to spread ketchup and mustard onto four pieces. Set aside.

Once patties are cooked through, scoop each one along with some onion onto one piece of bread. Top each with a pickle chip and then another bread piece (or the other way around, if you want to be fancy!). Let cool slightly, and then slide 'em into your mouth!

MAKES 1 SERVING

 For a pic of this recipe, see the first photo insert. Yay!

bursting burrito bowl

Sometimes a burrito is just better in a bowl, without the tortilla. Now don't get all technical on me and say it's not actually a burrito unless it's wrapped up in a tortilla. I'll cover my ears and scream, "LALALALALALA," until you stop talking. Just warning ya . . .

PER SERVING (entire bowl): 264 calories, 2g fat, 714mg sodium, 22.5g carbs, 5g fiber, 7g sugars, 39g protein

o Ingredients

⅓ cup sliced green and red bell peppers
¼ cup sliced onion
1 tablespoon canned diced green chiles
3 ounces cooked boneless skinless lean
    chicken breast, chopped
1½ cups shredded lettuce

¼ cup canned black beans, drained
    and rinsed
¼ cup shredded fat-free cheddar cheese
2 tablespoons pico de gallo
1 tablespoon fat-free sour cream

o Directions

Bring a skillet sprayed with nonstick spray to medium-high heat. Add bell peppers, onion, and chiles and, stirring occasionally, cook until onion is mostly translucent, about 3 minutes.

Add chicken and cook and stir until hot, about 2 minutes.

Place lettuce in a bowl and top with black beans and chicken-veggie mixture. Sprinkle with cheese, and then top or serve with pico de gallo and sour cream. Enjoy!

MAKES 1 SERVING

Extra, Extra!

Your leftover black beans are just begging to be used in our Santa Fe Cheesy Chicken Stir-Fry (page 26) or our Fiesta Bites (page 252)!

Extra, Extra!

Have an open can of chiles? Enjoy them in our Cheesy Crab 'n Chile Quesadilla (page 101), Chunky Veggie Pumpkin Chili (page 176), and Slow-Cookin' Mexican Chicken (page 182)!

chili cheese dog nachos

Maybe you never thought you could have nachos made with chili and hot dogs and cheese goo. That's what I'm here for . . . to provide you with fun things to chew that you thought you'd never be able to enjoy. These are CRAZY-FUN!

> **PER SERVING** (⅐th of recipe, 1 ounce chips with toppings): 218 calories, 3g fat, 674mg sodium, 36g carbs, 4.25g fiber, 4g sugars, 13g protein

○ Ingredients

2 cups low-fat turkey or veggie chili

3 fat-free or nearly fat-free franks, sliced into ½-inch pieces

One 7-ounce bag baked tortilla chips

½ cup chopped white onion

3 slices fat-free American cheese, cut into thin strips

½ cup fat-free sour cream

○ Directions

Preheat broiler.

Bring a skillet sprayed with nonstick spray to medium heat on the stove. Add chili and franks, and cook for about 3 minutes, until thoroughly heated. Set aside.

Arrange chips on an oven-safe platter or in a large casserole dish sprayed lightly with nonstick spray. Top chips first with chili-dog mixture and then with onion. Top evenly with cheese strips.

Place under the broiler for about 2 minutes, until cheese begins to melt and bubble. Top or serve with sour cream and eat!

MAKES 7 SERVINGS

 For a pic of this recipe, see the first photo insert. Yay!

chapter seven

Foiled Again . . .
and Again . . .
and Again

No one can explain exactly why wrapping stuff up in aluminum foil

and sticking it in the oven for a while to create tasty meals is so much fun . . . but it is. So. Much. Fun. FPRs (our little nickname for foil-pack recipes) have become insanely popular at HG. Here's an entire chapter featuring these clever and delicious meals.

Hungry Wrap

glaze-of-sunshine apricot chicken

Here's a sweet, tasty, fruity chicken dish that's super-fast. The entire family will FLIP over this one!

PER SERVING (½ of recipe, 1 cutlet with sauce): 233 calories, 3.5g fat, 274mg sodium, 13g carbs, 0g fiber, <0.5g sugars, 39g protein

o Ingredients

½ tablespoon light whipped butter or light buttery spread
1 tablespoon cider vinegar
½ tablespoon cornstarch
¼ cup sugar-free apricot preserves, room temperature
½ tablespoon dry onion soup mix
Two 6-ounce raw boneless skinless lean chicken breast cutlets
Optional: salt and black pepper

o Directions

Preheat oven to 375 degrees.

Place butter in a small microwave-safe bowl, and microwave until just melted. Set aside.

Combine vinegar and cornstarch in a bowl, and stir until cornstarch dissolves. Add preserves, melted butter, and soup mix. Mix well and set aside.

Place chicken in a large sealable plastic bag and, removing as much air as possible, seal the bag. Carefully pound chicken through the bag with a meat mallet or a heavy can, until it is uniformly about ½-inch thick.

Transfer chicken to the bowl with the preserves mixture, and flip until thoroughly coated.

Lay a large piece of heavy-duty foil on a baking sheet and spray with nonstick spray. Lay chicken flat in the center of the foil, and top with any remaining preserves mixture.

Fold together and seal the top and bottom edges of the foil, and then the side edges, to create a well-sealed packet.

Place baking sheet in the oven and cook for 25 minutes, or until chicken is cooked through.

Allow packet to cool for a few minutes, and then cut to release steam before opening it entirely. (Careful—steam will be hot.)

Plate chicken and top with any sauce remaining in the foil. If you like, season to taste with salt and pepper. Enjoy!

MAKES 2 SERVINGS

For a pic of this recipe, see the second photo insert. Yay!

For Weight Watchers *POINTS*® values and photos of all the recipes in this book, check out hungry-girl.com/book.

so-fancy fish pack

Yes, it really is fancy. Well, as fancy as a dish made in a folded piece of foil can be. And it tastes soooo amazing!

> **PER SERVING** (entire recipe): 205 calories, 4g fat, 412mg sodium, 6g carbs, 2.75g fiber, 3g sugars, 35g protein

o Ingredients

1 teaspoon light whipped butter or light buttery spread
½ teaspoon chopped fresh parsley
½ teaspoon crushed garlic
⅛ teaspoon salt
8 thin (or 6 thick) asparagus stalks, tough ends removed
6 ounces raw tilapia, cod, or similar type of white fish
2 slices lemon

o Directions

Preheat oven to 375 degrees.

In a small bowl, mix butter, parsley, garlic, and salt to form a thick paste. Set aside.

Lay a large piece of heavy-duty foil on a baking sheet and spray with nonstick spray. Line up the asparagus stalks side by side (like a raft) in the center of the foil. Lay the fish on top of the asparagus stalks.

Spread butter mixture evenly over the fish, and top with lemon slices. Fold and seal the top and bottom edges of the foil, and then the side edges, to create a well-sealed packet.

Place baking sheet in the oven and bake for about 15 minutes, until asparagus is tender and fish is cooked through.

Allow packet to cool for a few minutes, and then cut to release steam before opening it entirely. (Careful—steam will be hot.) Arrange fish and asparagus on a plate (use the lemon slices as a pretty garnish), admire, and eat!

MAKES 1 SERVING

mom-style creamy chicken 'n veggies

Total comfort food, people. Total. Comfort. Food. It's creamy and veggie-licious!

> **PER SERVING** (entire recipe): 307 calories, 4g fat, 881mg sodium, 26g carbs, 5.25g fiber, 10.5g sugars, 40g protein

○ Ingredients

¼ cup canned 98% fat-free cream of mushroom condensed soup

¼ cup fat-free sour cream

½ teaspoon chopped garlic

1 cup frozen cauliflower florets

½ cup frozen bite-sized mixed vegetables

¼ cup canned sliced mushrooms, drained

One 5-ounce raw boneless skinless lean chicken breast cutlet

Salt, black pepper, and additional spices, to taste

○ Directions

Preheat oven to 375 degrees.

In a bowl, mix condensed soup, sour cream, garlic, and salt. Add cauliflower, mixed veggies, and mushrooms, and stir to coat. Set aside.

Lay a large piece of heavy-duty foil on a baking sheet and spray with nonstick spray. Season chicken with salt, pepper, and any additional spices you like. Place chicken in center of the foil, and top with veggie mixture. Fold and seal the top and bottom edges of the foil, and then the side edges, to create a well-sealed packet.

Extra, Extra!

Make the most of your canned mushrooms by whipping up an Italian-Style Bacon Alfredo Bowl (p. 80), Sloppy Joe-chiladas (page 84), or a Happy Camper Cheeseburger Crumble (page 156)!

Place baking sheet in the oven and bake for about 35 to 40 minutes, until chicken is cooked through.

Allow packet to cool for a few minutes, and then cut to release steam before opening it entirely. (Careful—steam will be hot.) If you like, season to taste with pepper and additional salt. Now dig in!

MAKES 1 SERVING

 For a pic of this recipe, see the second photo insert. Yay!

HG Alternative!

Thaw your frozen veggies first, and reduce your cook time to 25 minutes or so!

chicken-with-a-kick pack

Not exactly sure what this dish is. A stew? A saucy taco filling? An entrée? However you describe it, it's completely DELICIOUS!

> **PER SERVING** (entire recipe): 245 calories, 2g fat, 923mg sodium, 24.5g carbs, 5g fiber, 4.5g sugars, 31.5g protein

o Ingredients

4 ounces raw boneless skinless lean chicken breast, chopped
⅓ cup canned tomato sauce
¼ cup canned seasoned black beans, lightly drained
¼ cup canned sweet corn kernels, drained
¼ cup chopped green bell pepper
1 teaspoon Tabasco Chipotle Pepper Sauce (or your favorite hot sauce)
Optional: salt

o Directions

Preheat oven to 375 degrees.

In a medium bowl, combine all ingredients and mix well. Set aside.

Lay a large piece of heavy-duty foil on a baking sheet and spray with nonstick spray. Scoop chicken mixture into the center of the foil. Fold and seal the top and bottom edges of the foil, and then the side edges, to create a well-sealed packet.

HG Tip!

Sodium-counters can shave about 480mg sodium off this recipe by using no-salt-added tomato sauce and fresh or frozen corn.

Place baking sheet in the oven and bake for 15 to 17 minutes, until chicken is cooked through.

Allow packet to cool for a few minutes, and then cut to release steam before opening it entirely. (Careful—steam will be hot.) This recipe is extra-saucy, so empty it right into a bowl. If you like, season to taste with salt. Dig in!

MAKES 1 SERVING

HG Alternative!

Give leftover corn a purpose in life . . . make Shrimped-Up Sweet Corn 'n Tomato Salad (page 115)!

caribbean shrimp packets

Tropical and pineapple-y, this pack is pure sweet shrimp-y yumminess!

PER SERVING (¼th of recipe): 267 calories, 3.5g fat, 341mg sodium, 35.5g carbs, 2g fiber, 26g sugars, 24.5g protein

o Ingredients

1 teaspoon cornstarch
2 tablespoons lime juice
1 pound large raw shrimp, peeled, tails removed, deveined
One 20-ounce can pineapple chunks in juice, drained
1 large red bell pepper, chopped
1 jalapeño pepper, seeded and finely chopped

½ cup chopped onion
1 tablespoon chopped garlic
¼ teaspoon cayenne pepper
¼ teaspoon salt, or more to taste
2 dashes black pepper, or more to taste
1 tablespoon light whipped butter or light buttery spread
2 tablespoons brown sugar (not packed)

o Directions

Preheat oven to 425 degrees.

In a small bowl, dissolve cornstarch in lime juice. Set aside.

In a large bowl, combine all other ingredients except for butter and brown sugar. Add lime juice mixture, stir well, and set aside.

In a small microwave-safe bowl, microwave butter until melted. Add butter to the large bowl and toss to coat. Set aside.

Lay a large piece of heavy-duty foil on a baking sheet and spray with nonstick spray. Place shrimp-veggie mixture in the center and spread it out a bit. Sprinkle brown sugar evenly over everything.

Place another large piece of foil on top. Fold together and seal all four edges of the two foil pieces, forming a well-sealed packet.

Place baking sheet in the oven and bake for about 15 minutes, until shrimp are opaque and cooked through.

Allow packet to cool for a few minutes, and then cut to release steam before opening it entirely. (Careful—steam will be hot.)

If you like, season to taste with additional salt and black pepper. Now EAT!

MAKES 4 SERVINGS

For more recipes, tips & tricks, food finds, and MORE, sign up for FREE daily emails at hungry-girl.com!

the rat(atouille) pack

This is SUCH a great dish. What a shame that Frank, Dean, and Sammy never got to try it . . .

> **PER SERVING** (entire recipe): 168 calories, 0.5g fat, 682mg sodium, 37.5g carbs, 10.5g fiber, 20g sugars, 7g protein

o Ingredients

1 cup cubed eggplant
½ cup chopped red bell pepper
½ cup sliced and halved zucchini
½ cup canned fire-roasted diced
    tomatoes, drained
½ cup coarsely chopped onion

¼ cup canned tomato paste
2 tablespoons finely chopped fresh basil
½ teaspoon chopped garlic
⅛ teaspoon salt, or more to taste
Dash crushed red pepper, or more to taste
Dash black pepper, or more to taste

o Directions

Preheat oven to 375 degrees.

In a medium bowl, combine all ingredients, and stir until veggies are evenly coated in tomato paste. Set aside.

Lay a large piece of heavy-duty foil on a baking sheet and spray with nonstick spray. Scoop veggie mixture into the center of the foil. Fold and seal the top and bottom edges of the foil, and then the side edges, to create a well-sealed packet.

Place baking sheet in the oven and bake for 30 minutes, or until veggies are tender.

Allow packet to cool for a few minutes, and then cut to release steam before opening it entirely. (Careful—steam will be hot.) If you like, season to taste with additional salt, crushed red pepper, and black pepper. Eat up!

MAKES 1 SERVING

crazy pineapple salmon teriyaki

I looooove teriyaki. This fish-in-a-flash pack is one of my favorites. If you're feeling adventurous, try adding more than a dash of cayenne—you'll love the sweet heat!

> **PER SERVING** (entire recipe): 347 calories, 15.5g fat, 349mg sodium, 22g carbs, 0.75g fiber, 19g sugars, 28.5g protein

o Ingredients

One 5-ounce salmon fillet
½ tablespoon thick teriyaki sauce with 20 to 25 calories per tablespoon
½ tablespoon sweet Asian chili sauce
2 pineapple rings packed in juice
Dash cayenne pepper, or more to taste

o Directions

Preheat oven to 375 degrees.

In a small bowl, mix teriyaki sauce with chili sauce. Set aside.

Lay a large piece of heavy-duty foil on a baking sheet and spray with nonstick spray. Place the salmon in the center, and top with the teriyaki-chili sauce. Flip salmon over to coat evenly on both sides.

Top fish with pineapple slices and sprinkle with cayenne pepper. Fold together and seal the top and bottom edges of the foil, and then the side edges, to create a well-sealed packet.

Place baking sheet in the oven and bake for about 20 minutes, until fish is cooked through.

Allow packet to cool for a few minutes, and then cut to release steam before opening it entirely. (Careful—steam will be hot.) YUM!

MAKES 1 SERVING

 For a pic of this recipe, see the second photo insert. Yay!

Extra, Extra!

Leftover pineapple? Make a Pizza Luau (page 10) or an Island Insanity Burger (page 130)!

Extra, Extra!

That sweet Asian chili sauce isn't just for salmon. Make Sweet 'n Sassy Boneless Hot Wings (page 126) and Sweet-Hot Steak Bites (page 188)!

happy camper
cheeseburger crumble

This is like a little pile of fast-food fun! Y.U.M.

> **PER SERVING** (entire recipe): 277 calories, 8g fat,
> 893mg sodium, 15.5g carbs, 2.25g fiber, 5g sugars, 34g protein

o Ingredients

4 ounces raw lean ground turkey
½ cup frozen potatoes O'Brien
¼ cup canned sliced mushrooms, drained
¼ cup shredded fat-free cheddar cheese
1 tablespoon ketchup

⅛ teaspoon garlic powder
⅛ teaspoon onion powder
Dash salt, or more to taste
Dash black pepper, or more to taste
Optional toppings: additional ketchup,
    mustard, relish

o Directions

Preheat oven to 375 degrees.

Combine all ingredients in a bowl, mix well and set aside.

Lay a large piece of heavy-duty foil on a baking sheet and spray with nonstick spray. Scoop turkey mixture into the center of the foil. Fold together and seal the top and bottom edges of the foil, and then the side edges, to create a well-sealed packet.

Place baking sheet in the oven and bake for 25 minutes, or until meat is browned and cooked through and potatoes are tender.

Allow packet to cool for a few minutes, and then cut to release steam before opening it entirely. (Careful—steam will be hot.)

Transfer to a bowl and use a fork to break the mixture up a bit. If you like, season to taste with additional salt and pepper.

Top with ketchup, mustard, and relish, or any of your favorite burger toppings. Grab a spoon, camper!

MAKES 1 SERVING

Extra, Extra!

For more fun with canned mushrooms, try an Italian-Style Bacon Alfredo Bowl (page 80), Sloppy Joe-chiladas (page 84), and Mom-Style Creamy Chicken 'n Veggies (page 146)!

Extra, Extra!

Potatoes O'Brien have many homes . . . like in our College Breakfast Burrito (page 70) and our Big Bowl of Breakfast (page 122)!

stuffed 'n squashed mushroom foil pack

Ahhhhh . . . These mushrooms are insanely HUMUNGOUS. And I LOVE huge food so much!

> **PER SERVING** (1 large stuffed mushroom): 92 calories, 2.75g fat, 447mg sodium, 11.5g carbs, 3.25g fiber, 4g sugars, 6.5g protein

o Ingredients

2 wedges The Laughing Cow Light Original Swiss cheese
½ teaspoon chopped garlic
½ teaspoon dried minced onion
⅛ teaspoon salt, or more to taste
Dash ground thyme, or more to taste

2 large portabella mushrooms
1 summer squash (yellow or green), ends removed, finely diced
½ tablespoon reduced-fat Parmesan-style grated topping

o Directions

Preheat oven to 375 degrees.

In a bowl, combine cheese wedges, garlic, onion, salt, and thyme. Mix until smooth. Set aside.

Remove mushroom stems and finely chop. Add chopped stems to the bowl, and set mushroom caps aside.

Add squash to the bowl and stir well, until veggies are coated in the cheese mixture.

Lay a large piece of heavy-duty foil on a baking sheet. Lightly spray both sides of the mushroom caps with olive oil nonstick spray, and place next to each other on the foil with the rounded sides down. Spoon veggie-cheese mixture into the mushroom caps—there will be a lot, so pack it in! Sprinkle with grated topping.

Place another large piece of foil over the caps. Fold together and seal all four edges of the two foil pieces, forming a well-sealed packet.

Place baking sheet in the oven and bake for 23 to 25 minutes, until mushrooms are tender.

Allow packet to cool for a few minutes, and then cut to release steam before opening it entirely. (Careful—steam will be hot.) If you like, season to taste with additional salt and thyme. Enjoy!

MAKES 2 SERVINGS

hustle 'n brussels foil-pack attack

Brussels sprouts are just tiny cabbages. And they're soooo cute! People who THINK they don't like 'em will be converted after trying this dish. Make it and see for yourself.

PER SERVING (½ of recipe): 182 calories, 2.75g fat, 513mg sodium, 35.5g carbs, 6.5g fiber, 5g sugars, 6g protein

o Ingredients

10 Brussels sprouts (or 14, if small), halved
4 baby red potatoes (about 10 ounces), cut to same size as halved sprouts
½ cup chopped onion
1 teaspoon olive oil
1 teaspoon dried rosemary
½ teaspoon chopped garlic
½ teaspoon coarse salt

o Directions

Preheat oven to 400 degrees.

Combine all ingredients in a bowl and mix well. Set aside.

Lay a large piece of heavy-duty foil on a baking sheet. Place veggie-potato mixture in the center of the foil, and spread it out a bit.

Place another large piece of foil over the veggie-potato mixture. Fold together and seal all four edges of the two foil pieces, forming a well-sealed packet.

Place baking sheet in the oven and bake for 30 to 35 minutes, until veggies are tender.

Allow packet to cool for a few minutes, and then cut to release steam before opening it entirely. (Careful—steam will be hot.) Serve and eat!

MAKES 2 SERVINGS

For Weight Watchers **POINTS®** values and photos of all the recipes in this book, check out hungry-girl.com/book.

fajitas in a foil pack

Nah, you don't need to stir-fry your fajita ingredients in a pan with lots of oil. That's SO 1990s! These mod fajita foil packs are A-mazing!

> **PER SERVING** (½ of recipe): 244 calories, 2.5g fat, 716mg sodium, 13g carbs, 3g fiber, 5.5g sugars, 41.5g protein

○ Ingredients

1½ tablespoons lime juice
1 teaspoon cornstarch
1 teaspoon garlic powder
1 teaspoon onion powder
1 teaspoon chili powder
½ teaspoon salt

⅛ teaspoon ground cumin
12 ounces raw boneless skinless lean
    chicken breasts, sliced into thin strips
1 bell pepper (any color), sliced
1 small zucchini, sliced into thin strips
Half an onion, sliced

○ Directions

Preheat oven to 375 degrees.

Combine lime juice and cornstarch in a large bowl, and mix until cornstarch dissolves. Stir in all the seasonings to form a thick paste. Add chicken and veggies and stir to coat. Set aside.

Lay a large piece of heavy-duty foil on a baking sheet and spray with nonstick spray. Spoon chicken-veggie mixture into the center of the foil and spread it out a bit. Place another large piece of foil over the chicken-veggie mixture. Fold together and seal all four edges of the two foil pieces, forming a well-sealed packet.

Place baking sheet in the oven and bake for 20 to 25 minutes, until chicken is cooked through and veggies are tender.

Let cool slightly. Using oven mitts, carefully flip packet over to mix contents, and then return to right-side-up. Cut packet to release steam before opening it entirely. (Careful—steam will be hot.) Enjoy!

MAKES 2 SERVINGS

📷 For a pic of this recipe, see the second photo insert. Yay!

For more recipes, tips & tricks, food finds, and MORE, sign up for FREE daily emails at hungry-girl.com!

do the cabbage pack!

Warning: Bacon and buttery deliciousness ahead! Who knew cabbage could be so decadent? WE DID!

> **PER SERVING** (¼th of recipe): 88 calories, 4.5g fat, 292mg sodium, 8g carbs, 2.5g fiber, 4.5g sugars, 5g protein

○ Ingredients

Half a head of green cabbage

1 small onion, sliced

2 tablespoons light whipped butter or light buttery spread

Dash salt, or more to taste

Dash black pepper, or more to taste

Dash paprika, or more to taste

¼ cup precooked real crumbled bacon

1 teaspoon chopped garlic

○ Directions

Preheat oven to 400 degrees.

Carefully remove the tough core from the cabbage using a sharp knife. Slice cabbage half into 4 thin wedges. Halve each wedge, leaving you with 8 "chunks."

Lay a large piece of heavy-duty foil on a baking sheet and spray with nonstick spray. Spread cabbage out in the center, and top with onion. Add butter in four evenly spaced dollops over the onion. Sprinkle with salt, pepper, and paprika. Top with bacon and garlic.

164

Place another large piece of foil over the veggies. Fold together and seal all four edges of the two foil pieces, forming a well-sealed packet.

Place baking sheet in the oven and bake for 30 to 35 minutes, until veggies are soft.

Let cool slightly. Using oven mitts, carefully flip packet over, allowing butter mixture to coat the veggies, and then return to right-side-up. Cut packet to release steam before opening it entirely. (Careful—steam will be hot.) If you like, season to taste with additional salt, pepper, and paprika. Mmmmm!

MAKES 4 SERVINGS

easy oven-baked s'mores-stuffed bananas

So fun and crazy-indulgent. We've tested this one on kids, husbands, friends, neighbors, and even the FedEx guy. It's a winner!!!

> **PER SERVING** (1 stuffed banana): 152 calories, 2.5g fat, 29mg sodium, 33g carbs, 3g fiber, 19g sugars, 1.5g protein

o Ingredients

2 tablespoons mini semi-sweet chocolate chips
1 sheet (4 crackers) low-fat honey graham crackers, crushed
4 small bananas, unpeeled, ripe yet slightly firm
¼ cup mini marshmallows
Optional topping: Fat Free Reddi-wip

o Directions

Preheat oven to 400 degrees.

Mix chocolate chips with graham cracker crumbs in a small bowl. Set aside.

Lay bananas on a flat surface, and cut a ¾-inch-deep slit lengthwise in each from top to bottom. Cut two small slits widthwise at the top and bottom of each banana, to make opening the fruit easier.

One at a time, use a fork to pry open bananas slightly and fill each with one-fourth of the chocolate-crumb mixture. Evenly distribute marshmallows among the bananas, pressing them into the openings.

Thoroughly wrap each banana in foil lightly sprayed with nonstick spray, ensuring there are no openings for filling to escape. Place bananas on a baking sheet.

Bake in the oven for 10 to 12 minutes, until bananas feel very soft when gently squeezed with an oven mitt.

Serve immediately with spoons for scooping the gooey mixture out of the peels or, if you prefer, transfer the mixture from each banana peel into a bowl. Top with Reddi-wip, if you like, and enjoy!

MAKES 4 SERVINGS

fruity fish fillet foil packs

Three ingredients, humans. Three ingredients.

> **PER SERVING** (½ of recipe): 204 calories, 3g fat, 358mg sodium, 10.5g carbs, 0.5g fiber, 6g sugars, 34g protein

○ Ingredients

Two 6-ounce fillets raw tilapia, cod, or any mild white fish
½ cup pineapple or mango salsa
¼ cup sliced red onion

○ Directions

Preheat oven to 375 degrees.

Lay a large piece of heavy-duty foil on a baking sheet and spray with nonstick spray. Place the fish fillets side by side in the center. Top fish evenly with salsa and onion.

Fold and seal together the top and bottom edges of the foil, and then the side edges, to create a well-sealed packet.

Place baking sheet in the oven and bake for about 15 minutes, until fish is cooked through.

Allow packet to cool for a few minutes, and then cut to release steam before opening it entirely. (Careful—steam will be hot.) Plate your fish filets and spoon any excess salsa on top. Mmmmm!

MAKES 2 SERVINGS

HG's Oven-to-Grill Foil-Pack Conversion Chart

Throw that foil pack on the grill! Here are a few pointers . . .

✳ The Temperature 411 ✳

OVEN	GRILL
375 degrees	Medium
400 degrees	Medium–High
425 degrees	High

✳ The Lowdown on Cook Time ✳

Cook your foil-pack on the grill for around half the time given for baking it in the oven (longer if the pack is full of veggies that you like on the soft side). Use long-handled barbecue tongs and oven mitts, and have a large plate or baking sheet to place the packet on afterward for easy transport away from the grill.

chapter eight

Crock Around the Clock

There's something oddly intriguing about tossing a slew of ingredients into a large pot

and cooking it slowly for hours and hours and hours. You just fill the pot, go about your day and, voilà, you've got something AMAZING once you get home. It's fun, people! But don't take my word for it—dust off your crock pot and get busy with these CROCK STARS! Pssst . . . You'll need a crock pot with a capacity of four quarts or more for the recipes in this chapter.

3pts

crazy-delicious seafood corn chowder

This chowder is so yum–tastic, I decided to write a little haiku poem about it.

Fat–free chicken broth
Morphed into deliciousness
Thank you, crab and corn!

> **PER SERVING** (1 generous cup): 138 calories, 1.5g fat, 553mg sodium, 16.5g carbs, 1.5g fiber, 5g sugars, 14.5g protein

Ingredients

Two 14.5-ounce cans (about 3 ½ cups) fat-free chicken broth
One 14.75-ounce can cream-style corn
Two 6-ounce cans lump crabmeat, thoroughly drained
One 6-ounce frozen fillet mild white fish (such as tilapia or cod)
2 cups (about 7 ounces) frozen cooked ready-to-eat shrimp

1 cup frozen sweet corn kernels
1 red bell pepper, chopped
½ cup finely chopped onion
½ cup plain light soymilk
½ teaspoon chopped garlic
½ cup instant mashed potato flakes
¼ cup fat-free sour cream
Optional: salt and black pepper

Directions

Place all ingredients except potato flakes and sour cream in the crock pot, and mix well. (Yup, that fish fillet goes in whole!)

Cover and cook on high for 3 to 4 hours or on low for 7 to 8 hours.

Stir to break up the fish fillet. Add potato flakes and sour cream, and stir very well. If you like, season to taste with salt and black pepper. Enjoy!

MAKES 9 SERVINGS

3 pts

slow-cookin' bbq chicken

This pulled chicken is FANTASTIC over salads, stuffed inside high-fiber tortillas or light buns with (rinsed) cole slaw, or eaten alone. It can do it all, really. I LOVE YOU, SLOW-COOKIN' BBQ CHICKEN!

PER SERVING (½ cup): 149 calories, 1g fat, 462mg sodium, 10g carbs, <0.5g fiber, 9g sugars, 22.5g protein

Ingredients

1 cup canned tomato sauce

½ cup ketchup

2 tablespoons plus 2 teaspoons brown sugar (not packed)

2 tablespoons plus 2 teaspoons cider vinegar

2 teaspoons garlic powder

1½ pounds raw boneless skinless lean chicken breasts, halved

Optional: crushed red pepper

Directions

Place all ingredients except chicken in the crock pot. Stir until mixed. Add chicken and coat well with the sauce.

Cover and cook on high for 3 to 4 hours or on low for 7 to 8 hours, until chicken is fully cooked.

Remove all the chicken and place it in a bowl. Shred each piece using two forks—one to hold the chicken in place and the other to scrape across the meat and shred it. Return the shredded chicken to the crock pot, and mix well with the sauce.

If you're serving a group, keep the crock pot on its lowest setting, so the chicken stays warm. If you like, season to taste with crushed red pepper. Eat up!

MAKES 7 SERVINGS

2 pts

chunky veggie pumpkin chili

Our friend canned pumpkin is at it again, adding fun, fiber, and flavor to this incredible chili. The taste is mellow but can easily be spiced up with extra cayenne or some hot sauce. Enjoy!

> **PER SERVING** (1 cup): 131 calories, 1g fat, 515mg sodium, 25g carbs, 6.5g fiber, 7g sugars, 6.5g protein

Ingredients

One 28-ounce can crushed tomatoes
One 15-ounce can pure pumpkin
2 teaspoons chopped garlic
½ tablespoon cayenne pepper, or
    more to taste
1 teaspoon chili powder
1 teaspoon pumpkin pie spice
¼ teaspoon salt, or more to taste
½ teaspoon ground cumin

One 14.5-ounce can diced tomatoes
One 15-ounce can chili beans (pinto beans
    in chili sauce), not drained
One 15-ounce can black beans, drained
    and rinsed
½ cup canned diced green chiles
2 cups chopped portabella mushrooms
1½ cups chopped zucchini
1½ cups chopped onion

Directions

Add crushed tomatoes, pumpkin, garlic, and all the seasonings to the crock pot. Mix well.

Add diced tomatoes, both types of beans, diced green chiles, and all the veggies. Stir thoroughly.

Cover and cook on high for 3 to 4 hours or on low for 7 to 8 hours. Enjoy!

MAKES 11 SERVINGS

 For a pic of this recipe, see the second photo insert. Yay!

Extra, Extra!

Canned chiles aren't just for chili. Use 'em in our Cheesy Crab 'n Chile Quesadilla (page 101), Bursting Burrito Bowl (page 136), and Slow-Cookin' Mexican Chicken (page 182)!

pump-up-the-jam cocktail weenies

At first I thought it might be a little weird to spend several hours cooking hot dogs that come pre-cooked. The recipe turned out so good, I realized I don't care about that at all . . . These little cocktail treats are a total crowd-pleaser!

> **PER SERVING** (3 cocktail weenies with sauce): 75 calories, 1.5g fat, 619mg sodium, 12.5g carbs, 0g fiber, 3g sugars, 6g protein

o Ingredients

1 cup chili sauce (the kind found by the ketchup)
¾ cup sugar-free grape or seedless blackberry jam
¾ cup very finely chopped onion
1½ teaspoons Dijon mustard
14 fat-free or nearly fat-free beef franks

o Directions

Place all ingredients except franks in the crock pot. Stir until completely mixed.

Cut each frank into thirds, leaving you with cocktail-sized franks. Add those to the pot, and gently mix to coat.

Cover and cook on low for 3 to 4 hours.

HG Heads Up!
It's important to use beef hot dogs in this recipe. Chicken, turkey, and veggie dogs don't work quite as well. You can try 'em if you like, but they're not nearly as good. Consider yourself alerted.

Stir well and then serve up franks with extra sauce on top!

MAKES 14 SERVINGS

 For a pic of this recipe, see the second photo insert. Yay!

dan-good cioppino

If you LOVE Dan–Good Chili (see *Hungry Girl: Recipes and Survival Strategies for Guilt–Free Eating in the Real World*), you will likely LOVE this tomato–based fish stew. It was created by my super–talented husband, Dan!

> **PER SERVING** (1 cup): 169 calories, 3g fat, 794mg sodium, 18.5g carbs, 1.25g fiber, 10.5g sugars, 16.5g protein

o Ingredients

Four 14.5-ounce cans (about 7 cups) low-fat creamy tomato soup

One 10-ounce can whole baby clams, drained

One 6-ounce can lump crabmeat, drained

8 ounces raw scallops, quartered

8 ounces raw shrimp, peeled, tails removed, deveined

2 bay leaves

4 cloves fresh garlic, crushed

½ teaspoon Worcestershire sauce

o Directions

Place all ingredients in the crock pot and stir.

Cover and cook on low for 3 to 4 hours.

Remove bay leaves. EAT!

MAKES 9 SERVINGS

HG Tip!

Amy's Organic Chunky Tomato Bisque is THE BEST soup to use in this recipe. THE. BEST. So find it!

5 pts

turkey mushroom surprise

LOVE this stuff . . . It's total comfort food! Try it over Tofu Shirataki noodles or a big bowl of steamed veggies. AWESOME!

PER SERVING (1 heaping cup): 226 calories, 8.5g fat, 670mg sodium, 10.5g carbs, 1g fiber, 2.5g sugars, 27.5g protein

Ingredients

1¼ pounds raw lean ground turkey
5 cups sliced mushrooms
1 onion, thinly sliced
One 12-ounce jar fat-free turkey gravy
1 tablespoon dry onion soup mix
1 tablespoon cornstarch

Directions

Add all ingredients except onion soup mix and cornstarch to the crock pot. Mix well, breaking up the ground turkey as you mix.

Cover and cook on high for 3 to 4 hours or on low for 7 to 8 hours.

Reduce heat to lowest setting. Sprinkle onion soup mix and cornstarch into the crock pot and stir until dissolved. Allow to sit, uncovered, for 5 minutes, or until the mixture has thickened slightly. Enjoy!

MAKES 5 SERVINGS

slow-cookin' mexican chicken

Cook up a crock pot full of this flavorful chicken, and then use it to make guilt-free tacos, quesadillas, wraps, salads, and more. Fiesta time!

PER SERVING (about ⅔ cup): 155 calories, 1.25g fat, 339mg sodium, 5.5g carbs, <0.5g fiber, 2.5g sugars, 27g protein

○ Ingredients

1 cup canned crushed tomatoes
½ cup jarred roasted red peppers
    packed in water, drained and chopped
¼ cup canned diced green chiles
1 tablespoon dry taco seasoning mix
½ tablespoon garlic powder

¼ teaspoon crushed red pepper, or more
    to taste
⅛ teaspoon black pepper, or more to taste
1½ pounds raw boneless skinless lean
    chicken breasts, halved
Optional: salt

○ Directions

Place all ingredients except chicken in the crock pot. Stir until thoroughly mixed. Add chicken and coat well.

Cover and cook on high for 3 to 4 hours or on low for 7 to 8 hours, until chicken is fully cooked.

Remove all the chicken and place it in a bowl. Shred each piece using two forks—one to hold the chicken in place and the other to scrape across the meat and shred it. Return the shredded chicken to the crock pot, and mix well with the sauce.

If you're serving a group, keep the crock pot on its lowest setting, so the chicken stays warm. If you like, season to taste with additional crushed red pepper, additional black pepper, and salt. Eat up!

MAKES 6 SERVINGS

Extra, Extra!

Take those additional chiles and shove 'em into a Cheesy Crab 'n Chile Quesadilla (page 101), a Bursting Burrito Bowl (page 136), or some Chunky Veggie Pumpkin Chili (page 176)!

Extra, Extra!

Hey, leftover roasted red peppers! How 'bout making your way into an Italian-Style Bacon Alfredo Bowl (page 80) or a Veggie-Packed Wrap Attack (page 118)?

1 pt

glaze-of-glory candied carrots

Who knew carrots could be as yummy as candy?! These are so sweet and delicious, you'll almost want to eat 'em for dessert. But that would be a little weird, so stick with the whole side dish plan, okay?

> **PER SERVING** (1 cup): 94 calories, 1.25g fat, 286mg sodium, 21.5g carbs, 3g fiber, 10g sugars, 1g protein

o Ingredients

One 32-ounce bag (about 6 cups)
   baby carrots
1 onion, sliced
1 red bell pepper, sliced
1 yellow bell pepper, sliced
¼ cup sugar-free apricot preserves
2 tablespoons brown sugar (not packed)
1½ tablespoons light whipped butter or
   light buttery spread

1 teaspoon cinnamon
½ teaspoon salt, or more to taste
¼ teaspoon nutmeg
1 tablespoon cornstarch
Optional: black pepper, cayenne pepper,
   ground ginger

o Directions

Place all veggies in the crock pot.

In a small dish, combine preserves, brown sugar, butter, cinnamon, salt, and nutmeg. Stir well. Top veggies in the crock pot with this mixture.

Use a large spoon to stir the contents of the crock pot up a bit. (Don't worry if the preserves mixture isn't completely distributed.)

Cover and cook on high for 3 to 4 hours or on low for 7 to 8 hours.

Once veggies are cooked, turn off the heat on the crock pot. Give contents a good stir, ensuring that the sauce is evenly distributed.

In a small bowl, combine cornstarch with 2 tablespoons cold water, and stir until cornstarch has dissolved. Add to crock pot and mix well.

Leave pot uncovered for 15 minutes to allow sauce to thicken. Stir and, if you like, add additional salt and optional ingredients to taste. Then enjoy!

MAKES 7 SERVINGS

3 pts

ez as 1-2-3-alarm turkey chili

Oooooh, an adjustable recipe?! Cool! Play around with the heat levels by using 1, 2, or 3 chipotle peppers. That's HG's definition of "spicy fun"!

PER SERVING (about 1 cup): 176 calories, 3g fat, 765mg sodium, 23g carbs, 5.5g fiber, 6g sugars, 13g protein

Ingredients

One 29-ounce can tomato sauce

One 14.5-ounce can diced tomatoes, drained

One 15-ounce can chili beans (pinto beans in chili sauce), not drained

One 15-ounce can red kidney beans, drained and rinsed

1 cup frozen sliced or chopped carrots

1 cup frozen sweet corn kernels

2 bell peppers (in different colors), chopped

1 large onion, chopped

1 to 3 canned chipotle peppers in adobo sauce, chopped, sauce reserved

2 teaspoons chopped garlic

1 teaspoon chili powder

1 teaspoon ground cumin

1 pound raw lean ground turkey

Salt, to taste

Optional topping: fat-free sour cream

Directions

Combine all ingredients except turkey and salt in a large bowl. Add 2 teaspoons adobo sauce from the canned chipotle peppers. Mix to combine and coat all beans and veggies with sauce.

Place turkey in the bottom of the crock pot and break up into small chunks. Pour chili mixture on top and mix.

Cover and cook on high for 3 to 4 hours or on low for 7 to 8 hours.

Stir to distribute turkey. Add salt to taste. If you like, top each serving with a little sour cream. Mmmmm!!!

MAKES 12 SERVINGS

4 pt

sweet-hot steak bites

This is an AWESOME party food, loved by all—especially men and hungry children. Watch out for those red pepper flakes. They can make these sweet beef chunks SUPER-HOT but soooooo delish!

PER SERVING (⅙th of recipe, about 6 "bites" with sauce): 196 calories, 4.5g fat, 254mg sodium, 18g carbs, 0.5g fiber, 15g sugars, 19.5g protein

o Ingredients

One 8-ounce can crushed pineapple packed in juice, lightly drained

⅓ cup sweet Asian chili sauce

½ teaspoon reduced-sodium/lite soy sauce

¼ teaspoon crushed red pepper, or more to taste

1 pound raw lean beefsteak filet, cut into about 30 bite-sized pieces

1 onion, finely chopped

o Directions

Place pineapple, chili sauce, soy sauce, and crushed red pepper in the crock pot. Mix well.

Add beef and onion and stir to coat.

Cover and cook on high for 3 to 4 hours or on low for 7 to 8 hours.

If you like, season to taste with additional crushed red pepper. Serve with excess sauce and toothpicks. Yum!

MAKES 5 SERVINGS

Extra, Extra!

Sweet Asian chili sauce, meet more recipes—Sweet 'n Sassy Boneless Hot Wings (page 126) and Crazy Pineapple Salmon Teriyaki (page 154)!

2 pts

hungry chick chunky soup

We set out to make a stew and ended up with this fantastic soup. Still, it's so thick and veggie-packed that it's definitely more of a meal than an appetizer. You'll want to hug your crock pot after tasting it. (Wait 'til it cools down, though!)

> **PER SERVING** (about 1 cup): 150 calories, 1g fat, 570mg sodium, 15g carbs, 4.25g fiber, 5g sugars, 20.5g protein

○ Ingredients

1½ pounds raw boneless skinless lean chicken breasts, halved

Two 14.5-ounce cans (about 3 ½ cups) fat-free chicken broth

One 15-ounce can white beans (such as cannellini), drained and rinsed

One 14.5-ounce can stewed tomatoes, drained

2 carrots, chopped

1 small onion, finely diced

2 cups bagged dry cole slaw

1 cup frozen peas

½ teaspoon salt

¼ teaspoon ground thyme

1 bay leaf

○ Directions

Place all ingredients in the crock pot and stir.

Cover and cook on high for 3 to 4 hours or on low for 7 to 8 hours, until chicken is fully cooked.

Remove the chicken pieces and place them in a bowl. Shred each piece using two forks—one to hold the chicken in place and the other to scrape across the meat and shred it. Return the shredded chicken to the crock pot, and stir into the soup.

Remove the bay leaf. Serve up and enjoy!

MAKES 10 SERVINGS

 For a pic of this recipe, see the second photo insert. Yay!

For Weight Watchers **POINTS**® values and photos of all the recipes in this book, check out hungry-girl.com/book.

chapter nine

Things That Go Blend

Blenders have many uses.

But mostly they're used to blend, puree, chop, and liquefy things. Okay, so that's pretty much ALL they do, but what more could you want from them, really? Prepare to press buttons and whip up slushies, smoothies, soups, shakes, and more. FYI, it is important to have a blender you LOVE, so locate   a good one if you haven't already. Just do it!

slush-puppy pineapple lemonade

This one's made with lots of fruit and a little bit of love. (It also has ice and sweetener packets, but those things don't sound as impressive for some reason.)

PER SERVING (entire recipe): 87 calories, 0g fat, 10mg sodium, 22.5g carbs, 1g fiber, 18g sugars, 0.5g protein

○ Ingredients

½ cup canned crushed pineapple packed in juice, not drained
1 tablespoon fresh lemon juice
2 no-calorie sweetener packets
1 cup crushed ice *or* 5 to 8 ice cubes

○ Directions

Place all ingredients in a blender. Add ½ cup water.

Blend on high until slush happens. Enjoy!

MAKES 1 SERVING

HG Tip!

Freeze your crushed pineapple in an ice cube tray for about 30 minutes. It'll make your drink slushier and ultimately more fantastic.

Extra, Extra!

An open can of pineapple means more guilt-free recipes . . . make some Cake on the Beach (page 88) and Teriyaki Shrimp 'n Slaw Stir-Fry (page 268)!

pretty-in-pink slushie drink

I love the name of this recipe. It just rolls off the tongue. Say it five times fast right now and see. It's fun. Did you do it???

> **PER SERVING** (entire drink): 125 calories, 0.5g fat, 11mg sodium, 31.5g carbs, 4g fiber, 21g sugars, 2g protein

o Ingredients

1 cup frozen unsweetened strawberries, slightly thawed
1½ cups chopped watermelon, seeds removed
¼ cup diet lemon-lime soda
1 no-calorie sweetener packet
1 cup crushed ice *or* 5 to 8 ice cubes
Optional garnish: mint leaves

o Directions

Place fruit in a blender. Blend on high for 1 minute, or until smooth.

Add soda, sweetener, and ice. Blend again until it reaches a slushie-like consistency.

If you like, garnish with a few mint leaves. Drink up!

MAKES 1 SERVING

cherry lemonade super-slushie

Cherries and lemonade are pretty AWESOME together. Want your slushie to be a little more like sorbet? Just freeze it for a while before enjoying it!

PER SERVING (entire slushie): 65 calories, 0g fat, 35mg sodium, 15g carbs, 2g fiber, 12g sugars, 1g protein

o Ingredients

Half a 2-serving packet (about ½ teaspoon) sugar-free lemonade powdered drink mix
⅔ cup frozen pitted dark sweet cherries
⅔ cup crushed ice or 3 to 5 ice cubes

o Directions

In a tall glass, dissolve drink mix in 1 cup cold water. Transfer to a blender.

Add cherries and ice and blend until mixed but still icy. Pour into the glass and enjoy!

MAKES 1 SERVING

cool 'n creamy fruit soup

This is sort of like a spoonable smoothie. It's reeeeeally good, so please don't let the whole "fruit soup" thing scare you.

> **PER SERVING** (½ of recipe, about 1 cup): 115 calories, <0.5g fat, 57mg sodium, 19g carbs, 1g fiber, 13.5g sugars, 8.5g protein

○ Ingredients

¾ cup red grapefruit segments (if packaged, packed in juice and drained)
5 strawberries
⅓ cup light vanilla soymilk
3 tablespoons Splenda No Calorie Sweetener (granulated)
¼ teaspoon cinnamon
¼ teaspoon vanilla extract
⅔ cup fat-free plain Greek yogurt

○ Directions

In a blender, combine all ingredients except yogurt. Puree until smooth.

Add yogurt and blend on low speed until just mixed.

Cover and refrigerate for at least 30 minutes. Pour into bowls and enjoy!

MAKES 2 SERVINGS

creamy dreamy portabella soup

You will TRULY be shocked when you taste this soup. It is so decadent and delicious, you may have a hard time believing the super-low stats. But don't doubt us. We're just magicians who reveal ALL of our secrets . . .

PER SERVING (⅓rd of recipe, 1 generous cup): 130 calories, 4g fat, 566mg sodium, 17.5g carbs, 3.25g fiber, 6g sugars, 7g protein

○ Ingredients

1½ tablespoons light whipped butter or light buttery spread

6 cups (about 1 pound) chopped portabella mushrooms

1 cup chopped onion

1 teaspoon chopped garlic

1 cup fat-free chicken broth

¼ cup fat-free nondairy liquid creamer

2 wedges The Laughing Cow Light Original Swiss cheese

¼ teaspoon salt, or more to taste

Optional: black pepper

○ Directions

Place butter in a large pot and bring to medium-high heat. Once butter has melted and coated the bottom of the pan, add mushrooms and onion. Stir thoroughly.

Sauté for 10 minutes, stirring occasionally. Add garlic and cook for 5 additional minutes.

Remove from heat and stir in broth and creamer. Allow to cool for several minutes and then transfer to a blender.

Place cheese wedges in a small microwave-safe bowl and microwave for 25 seconds. Mix with a fork until smooth. If needed, microwave for 10 additional seconds and mix again.

Add cheese to the blender and puree mixture until thoroughly blended and smooth. Add salt. If you like, season to taste with pepper and additional salt. Now heat, eat, and enjoy!

MAKES 3 SERVINGS

peachy-keen black bean soup

This soup is called "Peachy-Keen," but the recipe can be made with any fruity salsa. Sadly, the name "Pineappley-Keen" doesn't have quite the same ring to it, so PEACHY it is!

> **PER SERVING** (1 cup): 151 calories, 0.5g fat, 610mg sodium, 27g carbs, 7.25g fiber, 5g sugars, 7g protein

○ Ingredients

Three 15-ounce cans black beans, drained and rinsed

4 ½ cups (36 ounces) fat-free chicken or vegetable broth

One 12-ounce jar peach salsa or another fruity tomato-based salsa

1 teaspoon ground cumin

Optional toppings: fat-free sour cream, chopped cilantro, lime wedges

○ Directions

Pour about half of the beans into a blender. Add about half of the broth, half of the salsa, and half of the cumin (no need to be exact). Blend until mixture is smooth and fully pureed, and then transfer to a large bowl.

Repeat blending process with remaining ingredients, excluding optional toppings. Add that batch to the bowl, and give the mixture a good stir.

Cover and refrigerate for at least 1 hour (several hours is best), to allow soup to thicken and flavors to blend.

Once you're ready to serve, stir soup thoroughly. (Soup may separate in the fridge—this is okay!) Transfer soup to a pot or microwave-safe bowl, and heat on the stove or in the microwave until desired temperature is reached. If you like, top each serving with a dollop of sour cream, a sprinkle of cilantro, and a squeeze of lime. Mmmmm!

MAKES 8 SERVINGS

creamy caramelized onion bisque

This is one of those recipes that's so good, it may actually make you tear up. And trust us, those tears will be tears of sheer joy that have absolutely NOTHING to do with the onions in this recipe.

> **PER SERVING** (1 cup): 109 calories, 1g fat, 912mg sodium, 21g carbs, 1g fiber, 2.5g sugars, 4g protein

o Ingredients

1 tablespoon light whipped butter or
    light buttery spread
2 large sweet onions, chopped
4 large shallots, thinly sliced
2 tablespoons chopped garlic

½ teaspoon salt
Dash cayenne pepper, or more to taste
4 cups fat-free beef broth
¼ cup fat-free nondairy liquid creamer

o Directions

Heat butter in a large pot over medium-high heat on the stove. Once butter has coated the bottom of the pot, add onions, shallots, garlic, salt, and cayenne pepper. Onions may be piled high, but they'll cook down. Sauté for 10 minutes, stirring often.

Reduce heat to medium-low and cook for an additional 25 to 30 minutes, stirring occasionally, until onions are browned and caramelized.

Remove ½ cup of the caramelized onions, to be used to top soup, and set aside. Add broth to the pot and bring to a boil.

Reduce heat to medium-low. Let simmer for 15 minutes, stirring occasionally.

Remove pot from heat. Stir in creamer and let cool for several minutes.

Working in batches, puree onion mixture in a blender until smooth, 1 to 2 minutes per batch.

On the stove or in the microwave, heat soup to desired temperature. If you like, season to taste with additional cayenne pepper. Serve topped with the reserved caramelized onion. Now enjoy!

MAKES 5 SERVINGS

For a pic of this recipe, see the second photo insert. Yay!

For more recipes, tips & tricks, food finds, and MORE, sign up for FREE daily emails at hungry-girl.com!

chilla in vanilla milkshake

People who drink guilt-free vanilla milkshakes are 27 percent happier than those who don't. Everyone knows this . . .

> **PER SERVING** (entire shake): 162 calories, 2.25g fat, 127mg sodium, 28.5g carbs, 1g fiber, 8g sugars, 6g protein

○ Ingredients

½ tablespoon Coffee-mate Sugar Free French Vanilla powdered creamer
½ cup fat-free vanilla ice cream
½ cup light vanilla soymilk
2 no-calorie sweetener packets

⅛ teaspoon vanilla extract
1 cup crushed ice *or* 5 to 8 ice cubes
2 tablespoons Fat Free Reddi-wip
Optional topping: maraschino cherry

○ Directions

In a small bowl, dissolve powdered creamer in 1 tablespoon very hot water. Transfer mixture to a blender.

Add all other ingredients except Reddi-wip to the blender. Blend at high speed until completely mixed.

Pour into your favorite glass and top with Reddi-wip. If you like, finish it off with a cherry!

MAKES 1 SERVING

chocolate-covered-cherries freeze

There's something amazingly decadent about the sweetness of chocolate mixed with sweet 'n tart cherries. This one's a must–sip. FOR SURE!

PER SERVING (entire recipe): 160 calories, 4g fat, 163mg sodium, 28g carbs, 3g fiber, 21.5g sugars, 3.5g protein

Ingredients

One 25-calorie packet diet hot cocoa mix
1 tablespoon mini semi-sweet chocolate chips
1 no-calorie sweetener packet
12 frozen pitted dark sweet cherries
1½ cups crushed ice *or* 8 to 10 ice cubes
2 tablespoons Fat Free Reddi-wip

Directions

Place cocoa, chocolate chips, and sweetener in a tall glass. Add ¼ cup hot water and stir until ingredients dissolve. Add ¼ cup cold water and stir.

Pour cocoa mixture in a blender and add cherries and ice. Blend until smooth.

Pour into your glass and top with Reddi-wip. Enjoy!

MAKES 1 SERVING

 For a pic of this recipe, see the second photo insert. Yay!

slurpable split shake

Imagine sipping a delicious banana split thru a straw ... This thick, frozen concoction is truly one of the yummiest creations the HG blender's ever seen!

> **PER SERVING** (entire shake): 220 calories, 2g fat, 100mg sodium, 47g carbs, 4g fiber, 22g sugars, 5.5g protein

o Ingredients

3 frozen unsweetened strawberries

1 teaspoon sugar-free strawberry preserves

1 teaspoon Coffee-mate Sugar Free French Vanilla powdered creamer

1 small banana

½ cup light vanilla soymilk

¼ cup fat-free vanilla ice cream

1 no-calorie sweetener packet

1 cup crushed ice *or* 5 to 8 ice cubes

2 tablespoons Fat Free Reddi-wip

½ tablespoon Hershey's Lite chocolate syrup

Optional topping: maraschino cherry

o Directions

To make the topping, place strawberries in a small microwave-safe bowl, and microwave for 30 seconds, until mostly thawed. Mash thoroughly with a fork, mix in preserves, and set aside.

In another small bowl, combine powdered creamer with 1 tablespoon hot water, and stir until dissolved. Transfer to a blender.

To the blender, add banana, soymilk, ice cream, sweetener, and ice. Blend until smooth.

Pour into a tall glass and top with the strawberry mixture. Finish with Reddi-wip, chocolate syrup and, if you like, a maraschino cherry. Observe how beautiful it looks . . . then stir it up and enjoy!

MAKES 1 SERVING

For a pic of this recipe, see the second photo insert. Yay!

pumpkin-licious nog

Even if you're not a fan of eggnog, chances are you'll LOVE this stuff. And don't even think about limiting consumption of this delicious treat to holiday time. It's WAY too good for that . . .

PER SERVING (1 cup): 110 calories, 2g fat, 344mg sodium, 16g carbs, 2g fiber, 6.5g sugars, 6g protein

o Ingredients

5 cups light vanilla soymilk
1 small (4-serving) package sugar-free
    fat-free instant vanilla pudding mix
6 no-calorie sweetener packets
⅔ cup canned pure pumpkin

1 teaspoon rum extract
½ teaspoon ground nutmeg
½ teaspoon pumpkin pie spice
¼ teaspoon cinnamon
Optional topping: additional cinnamon

o Directions

In a blender, combine all ingredients and blend on high until mixed thoroughly. Cover and refrigerate for at least 2 hours to allow it to thicken.

If you like, top each glass off with a sprinkling of cinnamon. Enjoy!

MAKES 5 SERVINGS

HG Alternative!

If you want to make an alcoholic version of this drink, nix the rum extract and reduce the soymilk to 4½ cups—then add 5 ounces rum to the recipe. Each serving of the spiked stuff has 168 calories. Yay!

Shrimp & Grits . . . for Hungry Chicks!, p. 44

Swingin' Single Meals and Fast & for Two (or Three, or Four!)

Pizza Luau, p. 10

Three-Cheese Bacon-Apple-Bella Frittata, p. 42

Spring Chicken Skillet, p. 50

Girl-on-Grill Veggie Wraps, p. 58

Too-Beautiful Turkey Burger, p. 34

Pan-Fried Chicken Parm, p. 60

Planet Hungrywood Sweet & Cap'n Crunchy Chicken, p. 54

Te Quiero Tequila Shrimp, p. 64

Nuke It, Baby!

Cup o' Chocolate–Coconut Bread Pudding, p. 87

Italian-Style Bacon Alfredo Bowl, p. 80

Expresso Cake in a Mug, p. 89

College Breakfast Burrito, p. 70

Buff Chick Hot Wing Dip, p. 86

Sloppy Joe–chiladas, p. 84

Four Ingredients or Less

Stuffed Chick Cordon Bleu, p. 94

BFFs (Black Forest Fillo-cups), p. 105

Too-EZ Mac 'n Cheese, p. 98

Shrimp Cocktail Tacos, p. 100

Backyard BBQ Beef Cups, p. 96

Queen-of-the-Castle Sliders, p. 134

Sweet 'n Sassy Boneless Hot Wings, p. 126

Big Bowl of Breakfast, p. 122

Chili Cheese Dog Nachos, p. 138

toffee crush coffee shake

Wendy's swap alert!!! Candy, ice cream, and chocolate syrup? How can this thing have just 5.5g fat?! It's HG magic!

> **PER SERVING** (entire shake): 244 calories, 5.5g fat, 163mg sodium, 41.5g carbs, 1g fiber, 18g sugars, 5.5g protein

○ Ingredients

1 teaspoon Coffee-mate Sugar Free French Vanilla powdered creamer
¾ teaspoon instant coffee granules
1 no-calorie sweetener packet
½ cup fat-free vanilla ice cream
⅓ cup light vanilla soymilk

¾ cup crushed ice *or* 4 to 6 ice cubes
¼ cup Cool Whip Free, thawed
1 teaspoon Hershey's Lite chocolate syrup
One-third of a 1.4-ounce toffee chocolate bar, finely crushed into bits
Optional topping: Fat Free Reddi-wip

○ Directions

In a small bowl, dissolve powdered creamer, instant coffee granules, and sweetener in 2 tablespoons hot water. Transfer to a blender.

To the blender, add ice cream, soymilk, and ice. Blend briefly, until smooth, and then pour into a glass.

Gently fold in the Cool Whip, until uniform. Add chocolate syrup and toffee-chocolate bits (if you plan to top your drink with Reddi-wip, set a few candy bits aside), and stir gently to swirl them in.

If you like, top with Reddi-wip and sprinkle with remaining candy bits. Now dig in!

MAKES 1 SERVING

make-mine-mint
cookie-rific ice cream freeze

If creamy chocolate mint is your thing, you will FREAK over this shake. If you're not a fan of chocolate and mint together, skip ahead to the next recipe. It's for a pumpkin pie shake. Yay!

> **PER SERVING** (entire shake): 159 calories, 3.25g fat, 164mg sodium, 26.5g carbs, 1.5g fiber, 12g sugars, 6g protein

o Ingredients

½ pack 100 Calorie Packs Oreo Thin Crisps *or* ¾ sheet (3 crackers) chocolate graham crackers
1 teaspoon Coffee-mate Sugar Free French Vanilla powdered creamer
¼ cup fat-free vanilla ice cream
5 ounces (½ cup plus 2 tablespoons) light vanilla soymilk

2 no-calorie sweetener packets
¼ teaspoon peppermint extract
2 drops green food coloring
1 cup crushed ice *or* 5 to 8 ice cubes
Optional toppings: Fat Free Reddi-wip, additional cookie or graham cracker crumbs

o Directions

Lightly crush cookies or graham crackers and set aside.

In a small bowl, combine powdered creamer with 2 tablespoons hot water and stir to dissolve. Transfer to a blender.

To the blender, add ice cream, soymilk, sweetener, peppermint extract, food coloring, and ice. Blend on high for 45 to 60 seconds, until mixed thoroughly.

Pour into a tall glass and stir in the crushed cookies or graham crackers. If you like, top it all off with some Reddi-wip and cookie or graham cracker crumbs. Mmmmmm!

MAKES 1 SERVING

 For a pic of this recipe, see the second photo insert. Yay!

For Weight Watchers **POINTS**® values and photos of all the recipes in this book, check out hungry-girl.com/book.

pumpkin pie smoothie

This fun, frozen treat is great any time of day. Even in the early AM! Pumpkin pie for breakfast, anyone?!

PER SERVING (entire smoothie): 172 calories, 2g fat, 147mg sodium, 32g carbs, 5g fiber, 13.5g sugars, 6g protein

o Ingredients

¾ cup light vanilla soymilk
½ cup canned pure pumpkin
¼ cup Cool Whip Free, thawed
1 tablespoon sugar-free calorie-free
    vanilla syrup
½ teaspoon cinnamon
½ teaspoon brown sugar (not packed)

⅛ teaspoon pumpkin pie spice, or more
    to taste
2 no-calorie sweetener packets
1 cup crushed ice *or* 5 to 8 ice cubes
2 tablespoons Fat Free Reddi-wip
½ sheet (2 crackers) low-fat honey
    graham crackers, crushed

o Directions

Place all ingredients except Reddi-wip and crushed graham crackers in a blender. Blend at high speed until thoroughly mixed.

Pour the shake into a glass. If you like, add additional pumpkin pie spice. Top it off with Reddi-wip and crushed graham crackers. Mmmm!

MAKES 1 SERVING

HG Tip!

Torani makes the best sugar-free, calorie-free syrup out there. Visit the company's website to see where the syrups are sold near you or to order online!

Can't find syrup at the store (or don't feel like purchasing an entire bottle)? Just stop by Starbucks and order a shot of sugar-free vanilla syrup to go.

mud pie in the sky

FYI... DQ has nothing on HG. Forget fatty Blizzards. Forever.

> **PER SERVING** (entire recipe): 263 calories, 2g fat,
> 226mg sodium, 57g carbs, 3.5g fiber, 16g sugars, 7g protein

o Ingredients

½ to ¾ teaspoon instant coffee granules

½ teaspoon Coffee-mate Original Fat Free
    powdered creamer

2 teaspoons Hershey's Lite chocolate syrup

1 no-calorie sweetener packet

1 No Sugar Added Fudgsicle bar

¾ cup fat-free chocolate ice cream

¾ cup crushed ice *or* 4 to 6 ice cubes

½ pack 100 Calorie Packs Oreo Thin
    Crisps *or* ¾ sheet (3 crackers)
    chocolate graham crackers,
    slightly crushed

o Directions

In a small bowl, dissolve coffee granules and powdered creamer in 2 tablespoons warm water. Add syrup, sweetener, and 2 tablespoons cold water. Transfer mixture to a blender.

Cut the fudge pop into pieces (removing the stick), and add to the blender. Add ice cream and ice.

Blend briefly at medium-low speed until just mixed. Spoon mixture into a glass, and then stir in the cookie or graham pieces.

If needed, place in the freezer for 5 minutes to firm up. Then enjoy!

MAKES 1 SERVING

HG Tip!

Use ½ teaspoon coffee granules for a mild flavor, or use ¾ teaspoon for a full-on coffee kick!

chapter ten

Speedy
Sweeties

They're FAST, they're FUN, and they're SWEET.

Yup, they're SPEEDY SWEETIES. If parfaits, cookies, crepes, and various other dessert-like items are your thing, you'll be a huge fan of this chapter. Face it: Sweet stuff is delicious. Weeeee!

apple shakers

Confession time. While making these, we like to sing the directions to the tune of KC & The Sunshine Band's "Shake Your Booty." Read on to see what we mean . . .

PER SERVING (entire recipe): 102 calories, <0.5g fat, 2mg sodium, 27g carbs, 5g fiber, 19g sugars, 0.5g protein

o Ingredients

1 Fuji apple, cored and cubed
1 no-calorie sweetener packet
½ teaspoon cinnamon

o Directions

Place cubed apple in a sealable plastic bag. Add sweetener and cinnamon.

Seal bag and shake until evenly distributed. Meanwhile, sing, "Shake, shake, shake . . . Shake, shake, shake . . . Shake your apples! Shake your apples!"

MAKES 1 SERVING

4 points

dessert island parfait

As delicious and dessert-y as this is, it can TOTALLY be enjoyed for breakfast. Or for lunch—or as a snack. Don't pigeonhole this parfait, humans!

PER SERVING (entire parfait): 199 calories, 1g fat, 107mg sodium, 43.5g carbs, 2.75g fiber, 33.5g sugars, 8g protein

Ingredients

3 drops coconut extract

One 6-ounce container fat-free vanilla yogurt

Half a banana, chopped

¼ cup chopped mango

2 tablespoons Fat Free Reddi-wip

1 teaspoon shredded sweetened coconut

Directions

Add coconut extract to yogurt and mix well.

Spoon half of the yogurt into a glass, and then top with half of the banana and half of the mango. Repeat layering with remaining yogurt, banana, and mango.

Top with Reddi-wip and coconut shreds and enjoy!

MAKES 1 SERVING

super-simple
apple-cinnamon dessert crepes

This recipe is one of the most delicious and decadent creations we've ever whipped up. You can serve these caramel-drizzled treats to EVERYONE: adults, kids, fancy partygoers. Do NOT skip this one, people!

> **PER SERVING** (1 crepe, ½ of recipe): 117 calories, 1.25g fat, 226mg sodium, 22.5g carbs, 0.75g fiber, 10g sugars, 2g protein

o Ingredients

1 teaspoon Splenda No Calorie
    Sweetener (granulated)
¼ teaspoon cornstarch
⅛ teaspoon cinnamon
Dash salt
½ cup chopped apple
⅛ teaspoon lemon juice

1 tablespoon fat-free cream cheese,
    room temperature
½ cup Cool Whip Free, thawed
Two 9-inch ready-to-use dessert crepes
1 teaspoon fat-free or light caramel dip,
    room temperature

o Directions

In a small bowl, mix Splenda, cornstarch, cinnamon, and salt. Set aside.

Place apple in a microwave-safe bowl and sprinkle with lemon juice. Add Splenda mixture and stir to coat. Microwave for 1 minute, and then allow to cool slightly.

Add cream cheese to the apple mixture, and mix until evenly distributed. Fold in Cool Whip.

Lay crepes flat on a dry surface. Evenly distribute apple mixture between the crepes. Fold each crepe up envelope-style, first folding the sides in, and then folding the top and bottom toward the center.

Bring a skillet sprayed with nonstick spray to medium-high heat. Place crepes in the skillet with the seam-sides down. Cook until slightly browned, about 1 minute per side. (Flip carefully.)

Plate your crepes and drizzle with caramel dip. Try not to pass out as you dig in!

MAKES 2 SERVINGS

big black-and-white berry parfait

With layers of pudding and all kinds of berries, this is the BIGGEST parfait you'll ever eat for under 200 calories. And bigger is better when it comes to parfaits. Everyone knows that . . .

> **PER SERVING** (entire parfait): 196 calories, 3g fat, 371mg sodium, 45g carbs, 6g fiber, 11g sugars, 4g protein

○ Ingredients

1 Jell-O Sugar Free Vanilla Pudding Snack
⅓ cup chopped strawberries
⅓ cup blueberries
⅓ cup raspberries
1 Jell-O Sugar Free Chocolate Pudding Snack
¼ cup Fat Free Reddi-wip

○ Directions

In a bowl, combine vanilla pudding with all the berries. Gently mix to coat.

Spoon half of the chocolate pudding into a glass, and then top with half of the vanilla-berry mixture. Repeat with remaining chocolate pudding and vanilla-berry mixture.

Top with Reddi-wip and dive in!

MAKES 1 SERVING

 For a pic of this recipe, see the second photo insert. Yay!

gimme s'more sundae

How do you make s'mores even better?! Add ice cream and whipped cream. Doy! And mmmmmmmm!

> **PER SERVING** (entire sundae): 175 calories, 1.75g fat, 125mg sodium, 38g carbs, 2.25g fiber, 20g sugars, 4g protein

○ Ingredients

½ cup fat-free chocolate ice cream
2 tablespoons Jet-Puffed Marshmallow Creme, room temperature
½ sheet (2 crackers) low-fat honey graham crackers, lightly crushed
1 teaspoon mini semi-sweet chocolate chips
¼ cup Fat Free Reddi-wip

○ Directions

Spoon ice cream into a bowl and set aside.

Carefully place marshmallow creme in the bottom corner of a sealable plastic bag. Use scissors to snip a tiny hole from the outside of that corner, and squeeze 1 tablespoon of the creme (the rest will stick to the bag!) over your ice cream in a drizzle.

Top with crushed graham crackers and chocolate chips. Finish it all off with a generous squirt of Reddi-wip. Enjoy!

MAKES 1 SERVING

 For a pic of this recipe, see the second photo insert. Yay!

(3 pts)

caramel swirl cream puffs

OMG. These puffs may be THE BEST Hungry Girl dessert of all time. I tend to exaggerate (occasionally), but not this time. You MUST make these at some point over the next month. No excuses . . .

PER SERVING (1 "puff"): 121 calories, 3.5g fat, 266mg sodium, 22g carbs, 0g fiber, 6.5g sugars, 1.5g protein

○ Ingredients

1 package Pillsbury Crescent Recipe Creations Seamless Dough Sheet
2½ cups Cool Whip Free, thawed
3 tablespoons sugar-free fat-free vanilla instant pudding mix
1 Jell-O Sugar Free Chocolate Pudding Snack
¼ cup plus 2 tablespoons fat-free or light caramel dip, room temperature

○ Directions

Preheat oven to 375 degrees. Spray a 12-cup muffin pan with nonstick spray and set aside.

Roll dough out into a 12-inch by 9-inch rectangle. Using a knife or pizza cutter, cut into 12 squares.

Place each square of dough into a muffin cup, and press it into the bottom and up along the sides of the cup to form a little "dough cup."

Bake in the oven for about 12 minutes, until golden brown. Remove and let cool.

In a large bowl, combine Cool Whip and instant pudding mix. Stir until blended, thickened, and uniform.

Swirl chocolate pudding into the Cool Whip mixture, being careful not to over-stir.

Remove dough cups from the muffin pan and evenly distribute pudding mixture among them. Top each with ½ tablespoon caramel dip and use the end of a spoon or fork to swirl it into the creamy mixture. Serve and enjoy!

MAKES 12 SERVINGS

oatmeal raisin softies

These are 50 percent cookie, 50 percent muffin top, and 100 percent DELICIOUS!!!

> **PER SERVING** (1 medium-large cookie): 125 calories, 2.5g fat, 120mg sodium, 23.5g carbs, 2g fiber, 10g sugars, 3g protein

o Ingredients

¼ cup brown sugar (not packed)

2 tablespoons Splenda No Calorie
    Sweetener (granulated)

2 tablespoons light whipped butter or
    light buttery spread, room temperature

2 tablespoons no-sugar-added applesauce

2 tablespoons fat-free liquid egg substitute

¼ teaspoon vanilla extract

⅓ cup whole-wheat flour

¼ teaspoon baking soda

¼ teaspoon cinnamon

Dash salt

¾ cup old-fashioned oats

¼ cup raisins (not packed), chopped

o Directions

Preheat oven to 350 degrees.

In a bowl, combine brown sugar, Splenda, butter, applesauce, egg substitute, and vanilla extract, and mix thoroughly with a wire whisk.

Add flour, baking soda, cinnamon, and salt, and stir until completely mixed and smooth.

Add oats and raisins, and mix until both are thoroughly coated with batter.

Line a large baking sheet with parchment paper. Spoon batter onto the sheet in 6 evenly spaced mounds. Using the back of a spoon, spread and flatten batter into circles about 3½ inches wide.

Place baking sheet in the oven and bake for about 10 minutes, until a toothpick inserted into the center of a cookie comes out clean.

Remove from the oven, and allow cookies to cool for 1 minute on the sheet. Then slide parchment paper onto a cool surface, and let cool completely. Enjoy!

MAKES 6 SERVINGS

For a pic of this recipe, see the second photo insert. Yay!

peanut butter oatmeal softies

The average peanut butter cookie this size has more than 300 calories and 18 grams of fat. Why chew it? These Softies will kick a PB cookie craving STAT.

> **PER SERVING** (1 medium-large cookie): 170 calories, 6.25g fat, 169mg sodium, 23.5g carbs, 2.5g fiber, 7.5g sugars, 5.5g protein

○ Ingredients

¼ cup brown sugar (not packed)

¼ cup reduced-fat peanut butter, room temperature

2 tablespoons Splenda No Calorie Sweetener (granulated)

2 tablespoons light whipped butter or light buttery spread, room temperature

2 tablespoons no-sugar-added applesauce

2 tablespoons fat-free liquid egg substitute

¼ teaspoon vanilla extract

⅓ cup whole-wheat flour

½ teaspoon baking powder

Dash salt

¾ cup old-fashioned oats

○ Directions

Preheat oven to 350 degrees.

In a bowl, combine brown sugar, peanut butter, Splenda, butter, applesauce, egg substitute, and vanilla extract, and mix thoroughly with a wire whisk.

Add flour, baking powder, and salt, and stir until completely mixed and smooth.

Add oats and mix until they are thoroughly coated with the batter.

Line a large baking sheet with parchment paper. Spoon batter onto the sheet in 6 evenly spaced mounds. Using the back of a spoon, spread and flatten batter into circles about 3½ inches wide.

Bake in the oven for about 10 minutes, until a toothpick inserted into the center of a cookie comes out clean.

Remove from the oven, and allow cookies to cool for 1 minute on the sheet. Then slide parchment paper onto a cool surface, and let cool COMPLETELY. (Really, they taste best once they've totally cooled.) Enjoy!

MAKES 6 SERVINGS

HG Alternative!

If you can find Better'n Peanut Butter, use it. If you do, each Softie will have 140 calories, 3.25g fat, and 2g fiber. Woohoo!

For more recipes, tips & tricks, food finds, and MORE, sign up for FREE daily emails at hungry-girl.com!

upside-down personal key lime pies

This recipe makes FIVE individual servings. No need to worry about cutting oversized and over-caloried slices. Whip up a batch on Monday, and enjoy personal-sized pies all week . . .

> **PER SERVING** (1 "pie"): 82 calories, 1g fat, 103mg sodium, 15g carbs, <0.5g fiber, 5g sugars, 1g protein

○ Ingredients

One 4-serving package (or half an 8-serving package) Jell-O Sugar Free
    Lime Gelatin dessert mix
1 no-calorie sweetener packet
1½ tablespoons lemon juice
¼ teaspoon vanilla extract
2 cups Cool Whip Free, thawed
2 sheets (8 crackers) low-fat honey graham crackers, lightly crushed

○ Directions

In a medium bowl, combine 1 cup boiling water with gelatin mix and sweetener. Stir for at least 2 minutes, until completely dissolved.

Mix in lemon juice, vanilla extract, and ½ cup cold water. Refrigerate for about 45 minutes, until slightly thickened but still mixable.

Stir in the Cool Whip. Whisk until thoroughly blended. Divide mixture among 5 small bowls. Refrigerate until firm, at least 3 hours.

Once ready to serve, evenly distribute crushed graham crackers over the pies. Eat up!

MAKES 5 SERVINGS

hot fudge 'n brownie blitz

Whip up your very own brownie sundae. It's a delicious little after-dinner project. Weeeee!

> **PER SERVING** (entire sundae): 190 calories, 2g fat, 134mg sodium, 40g carbs, 2.5g fiber, 23.5g sugars, 4.5g protein

○ Ingredients

1 tablespoon traditional fudge brownie mix
½ teaspoon fat-free liquid egg substitute
½ cup fat-free chocolate ice cream
1 teaspoon mini semi-sweet chocolate chips
2 teaspoons Hershey's Lite chocolate syrup
2 tablespoons Fat Free Reddi-wip

○ Directions

In a small microwave-safe bowl, combine brownie mix, egg substitute, and ½ teaspoon water, and mix well. Microwave for 45 seconds. Let stand for 5 minutes.

Using a fork, break up and crumble brownie into bits. (You can use your fingers, too—just make sure your hands are clean!)

Spoon ice cream into a small bowl, and top with brownie bits. Set aside.

Place chocolate chips in a small microwave-safe bowl, and cover with syrup. Microwave for 45 seconds. Mix well and pour over the sundae.

Top with Reddi-wip and dig in!!!

MAKES 1 SERVING

 For a pic of this recipe, see the second photo insert. Yay!

upside-down pineapple crush

HG subscriber Molly inspired us to create this fantastic, creamy, pudding-and-wafer-packed dessert. Yay, Molly!

PER SERVING (1/8th of dessert, about 2/3 cup): 135 calories, 0.5g fat, 296mg sodium, 30g carbs, 0.5g fiber, 18.5g sugars, 2.5g protein

○ Ingredients

One 20-ounce can crushed pineapple packed in juice, not drained
1 large (6-serving) package fat-free sugar-free vanilla instant pudding mix
2 cups fat-free vanilla yogurt
1 cup Cool Whip Free, thawed
16 Reduced Fat Nilla Wafers, crushed
Optional topping: Fat Free Reddi-wip

○ Directions

Combine undrained pineapple, pudding mix, yogurt, and Cool Whip in a bowl. Mix until uniform and free of lumps.

Pour into a large pie pan. Refrigerate for 1 hour, or until ready to serve.

Top dish evenly with crushed Nilla Wafers just before serving. If you like, finish off each serving with a squirt of Reddi-wip. Enjoy!

MAKES 8 SERVINGS

that's hazel-nuts! cocoa supreme

Sorry, Starbucks. We think 450 calories is WAY too much for a mug of cocoa. We like our version better. (Just being honest.)

> **PER SERVING** (entire recipe): 114 calories, 5g fat, 173mg sodium, 15.5g carbs, 2.5g fiber, 9g sugars, 3g protein

○ Ingredients

One 25-calorie packet diet hot cocoa mix
2 teaspoons Coffee-mate Sugar Free Hazelnut powdered creamer
2 teaspoons unsweetened cocoa powder
2 teaspoons mini semi-sweet chocolate chips
¼ cup Fat Free Reddi-wip
Optional garnish: additional unsweetened cocoa powder

○ Directions

Place all ingredients except Reddi-wip in a mug. Add 1 cup very hot water, and stir until ingredients are fully dissolved, melted, and combined.

Top with Reddi-wip and, if you like, sprinkle with additional cocoa powder. Consume as soon as you can without burning your tongue!

MAKES 1 SERVING

scoopable creamsicle crush pie

Orange-y, vanilla goodness is only a few stirs, chops, and sprinkles away!

PER SERVING (⅛th of dessert, about ⅔ cup): 112 calories,
0.5g fat, 284mg sodium, 25g carbs, 0.5g fiber, 15.5g sugars, 3g protein

o Ingredients

Two 10.5-ounce cans mandarin orange segments packed in juice, not drained
1 large (6-serving) package fat-free sugar-free vanilla instant pudding mix
2 cups fat-free vanilla yogurt
1 cup Cool Whip Free, thawed
10 Reduced Fat Nilla Wafers, crushed
Optional topping: Fat Free Reddi-wip

o Directions

Pour the juice from the oranges into a large bowl. Add pudding mix, yogurt, and Cool Whip, and mix until uniform and free of lumps. Set aside.

Place 8 orange segments in a small bowl, to be used later for topping, and refrigerate.

Roughly chop all the remaining oranges, and gently mix them into the pudding mixture.

Pour contents of the bowl into a large pie pan. Refrigerate for 1 hour, or until ready to serve.

Just before serving, sprinkle crushed Nilla Wafers over the majority of the top of the dish, leaving an uncovered circle in the center.

Arrange reserved orange segments decoratively in the circle. If you like, finish off each serving with a squirt of Reddi-wip. Enjoy!

MAKES 8 SERVINGS

For a pic of this recipe, see the second photo insert. Yay!

For Weight Watchers *POINTS*® values and photos of all the recipes in this book, check out hungry-girl.com/book.

chapter eleven

EZ &
Crowd-Pleasy

The recipes populating this chapter are GREAT for parties and get-togethers.

Family members, party-goers, book-club attendees, etc., will LOVE them. We know because they've all been tested. Often. By very picky people.

oven-baked omelette lasagna

This thing is HUGE, and the serving size is tremendous, too. If you like LARGE portions for SMALL amounts of calories, this dish is your dream come true.

> **PER SERVING** (⅛th of recipe): 182 calories, 4.25g fat, 664mg sodium, 12g carbs, 2.25g fiber, 5g sugars, 23g protein

o Ingredients

2 large zucchini

1 large portabella mushroom

1 onion, sliced

1 cup shredded part-skim mozzarella cheese

4 cups fat-free liquid egg substitute

1 teaspoon baking powder

1 teaspoon chopped garlic

1 teaspoon Italian seasoning

¼ teaspoon salt

2 cups roughly chopped fresh spinach leaves

½ cup roughly chopped fresh basil

2 firm plum tomatoes

2 tablespoons reduced-fat Parmesan-style
   grated topping

o Directions

Preheat oven to 425 degrees.

Cut zucchini lengthwise at an angle into ½-inch-thick slices. Remove stem from the mushroom, and cut cap into ½-inch-thick slices. Chop stem and set aside.

Bring a large skillet sprayed with nonstick spray to medium-high heat on the stove. Working in batches, cook zucchini, mushroom slices, and onion for 3 minutes per side, removing skillet from heat and re-spraying it between batches.

Spray a 9-inch by 13-inch baking pan with nonstick spray, making sure to spray the sides as well as the bottom. Lay cooked veggies along the bottom of the pan. Sprinkle evenly with mozzarella cheese. Set aside.

In a large bowl, combine egg substitute, baking powder, garlic, Italian seasoning, and salt. Whisk until smooth and fluffy, about 2 minutes. Stir in spinach, basil, and chopped mushroom stem. Pour mixture over the cheese layer in the baking pan.

Place baking pan in the oven and bake for 20 minutes, until firm and lightly browned at the edges. Meanwhile, slice tomatoes and place on a layer of paper towels to absorb some of the moisture.

Carefully remove baking pan from the oven and top evenly with tomatoes. Sprinkle with grated topping.

Return it to the oven and cook for 5 minutes longer. Allow to cool slightly, and then dig in!

MAKES 6 SERVINGS

 For a pic of this recipe, see the second photo insert. Yay!

perfect pumpkin bread

This pumpkin bread IS perfect. And it's great any time of year, so don't let anyone tell you it's a "fall food"!

> **PER SERVING** (1 thick slice): 143 calories, 0.5g fat, 281mg sodium, 31g carbs, 4.5g fiber, 9g sugars, 5g protein

o Ingredients

1¼ cups whole-wheat flour

¼ cup all-purpose flour

½ cup Splenda No Calorie Sweetener (granulated)

¼ cup brown sugar (not packed)

2¼ teaspoons baking powder

1½ teaspoons cinnamon

½ teaspoon salt

⅓ teaspoon pumpkin pie spice

One 15-ounce can pure pumpkin

½ cup fat-free liquid egg substitute

1 teaspoon vanilla extract

¼ cup sweetened dried cranberries or raisins (not packed), chopped

o Directions

Preheat oven to 350 degrees.

In a large bowl, combine both types of flour, Splenda, brown sugar, baking powder, cinnamon, salt, and pumpkin pie spice.

In a medium bowl, mix pumpkin, egg substitute, and vanilla extract (all the wet ingredients). Add this mixture to the bowl with the dry ingredients, and stir until just blended.

Slowly sprinkle chopped cranberries or raisins into the batter, making sure they don't all stick together, and mix to distribute them.

Spoon batter into a large loaf pan sprayed with nonstick spray. Bake in the oven for about 50 minutes, until the top of the loaf is firm to the touch. (Bread may be moist inside. This doesn't mean it's undercooked.) Allow to cool, and then cut into 8 slices. Enjoy!

MAKES 8 SERVINGS

HG Alternative!

To make this bread into muffins, evenly distribute the batter among 8 cups of a muffin pan lined with baking cups and/or sprayed with nonstick spray. Cook for 35 minutes at 350 degrees, let cool, and enjoy!

fruity bruschetta

Don't knock the idea of fruit bruschetta until you try it. This stuff is so good, it will probably make you squeal when you taste it.

> **PER SERVING** (2 pieces): 78 calories, 1.5g fat, 92mg sodium, 15g carbs, 1g fiber, 6.5g sugars, 1.5g protein

o Ingredients

1 mango, diced
1 small banana, diced
½ cup diced strawberries
1 French baguette about 2 inches in thickness and at least 6 inches long

2 tablespoons light whipped butter or light buttery spread
½ teaspoon cinnamon
2 no-calorie sweetener packets
⅓ cup fat-free fruit-flavored yogurt (your choice)

o Directions

Preheat broiler.

Stir all fruit together in a bowl. Cover and refrigerate.

Using a sharp serrated knife, carefully cut sixteen ¼-inch-thick slices from the baguette. (Save any remaining bread for another use.) Lay bread slices in a single layer on a large baking sheet. Set aside.

Place butter in a small microwave-safe bowl and microwave until just melted. Add cinnamon and sweetener and mix well. Brush the tops of the bread slices with butter mixture.

Place the baking sheet about 5 inches beneath the broiler and let broil for 3 minutes, or until tops are slightly bubbly.

Evenly distribute chilled fruit among the bread slices. Top each with a teaspoon of yogurt.

Enjoy!

MAKES 8 SERVINGS

exploding chicken taquitos

Gotta be honest, I was hesitant to try out canned chicken in this recipe. (I was a little scared of it!) Turns out, I had nothing to worry about. It ROCKS. And yes, they actually do explode. But in a good and non-dangerous way. I promise . . .

> **PER SERVING** (2 taquitos): 197 calories, 2.5g fat, 594mg sodium, 22.5g carbs, 3g fiber, 2g sugars, 20.5g protein

○ Ingredients

One 9.75-ounce (or 10-ounce) can 98% fat-free chunk
   white chicken breast in water, drained and flaked
½ cup salsa
⅓ cup shredded fat-free cheddar cheese
¼ teaspoon dry taco seasoning mix
Eight 6-inch corn tortillas
Optional dips: red enchilada sauce, additional salsa,
   fat-free sour cream

○ Directions

Preheat oven to 375 degrees.

In a medium bowl, combine the chicken and salsa, and mix thoroughly. Cover and refrigerate for 15 minutes.

Remove chicken mixture from the fridge, and drain any excess liquid. Add cheese and taco seasoning, and mix to combine. This is your filling. Set aside.

Prepare a baking sheet by spraying with nonstick spray, and set it aside.

Dampen two paper towels, and place tortillas between them. Microwave for about 1 minute, until tortillas are warm and pliable.

Take one tortilla (keep the rest between the paper towels), spray both sides lightly with nonstick spray, and lay it flat on a clean dry surface. Spoon about 2 heaping tablespoons of filling onto the tortilla. Spread it evenly across the entire surface, and roll tortilla up tightly, so that you have a cigar-shaped tube. Secure with toothpicks and place seam-side down on the baking sheet. Repeat with remaining tortillas and filling.

Bake in the oven for 14 to 16 minutes, until crispy. Allow taquitos to cool for 5 minutes. If you like, dunk in enchilada sauce, salsa, or sour cream!

MAKES 4 SERVINGS

📷 For a pic of this recipe, see the second photo insert. Yay!

tomato bacon tarts

Flaky pastry dough with creamy bacon and tomato?! How on EARTH can these be guilt-free?

> **PER SERVING** (1 tart): 104 calories, 5.25g fat, 409mg sodium, 12g carbs, <0.5g fiber, 3g sugars, 3.5g protein

o Ingredients

8 slices center-cut bacon or turkey bacon

2 small tomatoes, deseeded, finely chopped, patted dry

1 small onion, finely chopped

¾ cup fat-free mayonnaise

1 teaspoon garlic powder

1 package Pillsbury Crescent Recipe Creations Seamless Dough Sheet

2 tablespoons reduced-fat Parmesan-style grated topping

o Directions

Preheat oven to 375 degrees. Spray a 12-cup muffin pan with nonstick spray and set aside.

Bring a large skillet sprayed with nonstick spray to medium-high heat on the stove. Add bacon and cook until crispy. Remove from heat and let cool.

Add tomatoes, onion, mayo, and garlic powder to a bowl. Once cool enough to handle, chop bacon and add to the bowl as well. Mix thoroughly and set aside.

Roll dough out into a 12-inch by 9-inch rectangle. Using a knife or pizza cutter, cut into 12 squares.

Place each square of dough into a muffin cup, and press it into the bottom and up along the sides of the cup to form a little "dough cup" for the bacon mixture.

Evenly distribute mixture among the cups. Sprinkle ½ teaspoon grated topping over each cup.

Bake in the oven for about 12 minutes, until golden brown. Let cool slightly, and then enjoy!

MAKES 12 SERVINGS

corndog millionaire muffins

Yes, I shoved no-guilt hot dogs into low-calorie corn muffins. It's a VERY HG thing to do, and it's REALLY pretty delicious. So try 'em before you start pointing and laughing . . .

PER SERVING (1 muffin): 160 calories, 2g fat, 636mg sodium, 27g carbs, 1g fiber, 6.5g sugars, 9g protein

o Ingredients

⅔ cup all-purpose flour

½ cup yellow cornmeal

2 ½ tablespoons Splenda No Calorie
    Sweetener (granulated)

2 ½ tablespoons granulated sugar

1½ teaspoons baking powder

¼ teaspoon salt

1 cup canned cream-style corn

½ cup fat-free liquid egg substitute

½ cup fat-free sour cream

7 fat-free or nearly fat-free franks

o Directions

Preheat oven to 375 degrees.

Combine flour, cornmeal, Splenda, sugar, baking powder, and salt in a large bowl. Mix well and set aside. In a separate small bowl, mix corn, egg substitute, and sour cream. Stir thoroughly. Add contents of the small bowl to the large one, and stir until completely mixed.

Cut 2 franks in half, leaving you with 4 cocktail-sized franks. Cut each of the halves into 6 pieces, leaving you with 24 "coins." Set aside. (You'll use these to top the muffins.)

Chop the remaining franks into very small pieces. Add those to the large bowl, and stir until they are integrated into the batter.

Line 8 cups of a 12-cup muffin pan with baking cups and/or spray with nonstick spray. Evenly distribute batter among the 8 cups. Top each muffin with 3 of the frank "coins."

Bake in the oven for 15 to 20 minutes, until a toothpick inserted into the center of a muffin comes out clean. Allow to cool and then enjoy!

MAKES 8 SERVINGS

For a pic of this recipe, see the second photo insert. Yay!

For Weight Watchers **POINTS**® values and photos of all the recipes in this book, check out hungry-girl.com/book.

fiesta bites

Each one of these things is a little party exploding with Mexican flavor and fun. Weeeeeeee!

> **PER SERVING** (1 "bite"): 55 calories, 0.5g fat, 190mg sodium, 6g carbs, 0.5g fiber, 0.5g sugars, 6g protein

o Ingredients

12 small square wonton wrappers

2 tablespoons taco sauce

1 tablespoon fat-free cream cheese, room temperature

1 teaspoon dry taco seasoning mix

One 9.75-ounce (or 10-ounce) can 98% fat-free chunk white chicken breast in water, drained and flaked

¼ cup canned black beans, drained and rinsed

¼ cup corn, thawed from frozen

¼ cup shredded fat-free cheddar cheese

1 plum tomato, chopped

Optional: salt and black pepper

o Directions

Preheat oven to 350 degrees.

Spray a 12-cup muffin pan with nonstick spray. Place each wonton wrapper into a cup of the muffin pan, and press it into the bottom and sides.

Lightly spray wrappers with nonstick spray. Bake in the oven for about 4 minutes, until the corners begin to brown. Leaving the oven on, set muffin pan aside to cool.

Mix taco sauce, cream cheese, and taco seasoning together in a bowl. Add chicken and stir until coated. Add beans, corn, and cheddar cheese, and stir well. If you like, season to taste with salt and pepper.

Evenly distribute mixture into the wonton shells, about 2 tablespoons each. Return pan to the oven and bake for about 8 minutes, until the chicken mixture is hot.

Once cool enough to handle, remove the filled wonton shells and top evenly with tomato. Serve and enjoy!

MAKES 12 SERVINGS

Extra, Extra!

Looking for more to make with canned black beans? Whip up the Santa Fe Cheesy Chicken Stir-Fry on page 26 or the Bursting Burrito Bowl on page 136!

yumbo gumbo

This soup is hearty, thick, delicious, and CRAMMED with shrimp. There's no way anyone would ever believe how low in calories and fat grams it is.

> **PER SERVING** (1 cup): 133 calories, 1.25g fat, 710mg sodium, 14g carbs, 2.5g fiber, 7g sugars, 17g protein

o Ingredients

½ cup chopped green bell pepper
½ cup chopped red bell pepper
½ cup chopped onion
One 14.5-ounce can stewed tomatoes, not drained
1 cup Spicy Hot V8 vegetable juice
1 tablespoon cornstarch
1 cup frozen cut okra
2 teaspoons dry Cajun seasoning, or more to taste

1 teaspoon Frank's RedHot Original Cayenne Pepper Sauce, or more to taste
8 ounces raw shrimp, peeled, tails removed, deveined
8 ounces white crabmeat (about two 6-ounce cans drained)
Black pepper, to taste

o Directions

Bring a large pot sprayed with nonstick spray to medium heat. Add bell peppers and onion. Stirring occasionally, cook for about 3 minutes, until tender.

Add tomatoes, vegetable juice, and cornstarch. Stir well, making sure cornstarch dissolves completely. Cook until mixture begins to bubble. Add okra, Cajun seasoning, and hot sauce. Stir and bring mixture to a boil.

Reduce heat to low. Cover and let simmer for 10 minutes.

Add shrimp, and continue to simmer until shrimp are opaque and cooked through, about 3 to 4 minutes. Add crabmeat and ¾ cup water. Raise heat to medium, and return to a boil.

Remove pot from heat, cover, and let thicken for 5 minutes. Season to taste with black pepper. If you like, add a little more Cajun seasoning and Frank's RedHot. Enjoy!

MAKES 5 SERVINGS

HG Alternative!

For a more traditional gumbo, add ¾ cup cooked brown rice to the pot just before you cover it during the last step. Each serving will then have 165 calories, 1.5g fat, 710mg sodium, 21g carbs, 3g fiber, 7g sugars, and 17.5g protein.

sloppy franks

Sloppy Joes have nothing on these. NO–THING. This one's a hit with men and kids, too. So don't hog the Sloppy Franks, people!

> **PER SERVING** (1 "sloppy frank"): 170 calories, 2g fat, 1,097mg sodium, 31.5g carbs, 3.5g fiber, 8g sugars, 10g protein

o Ingredients

½ cup chopped onion
½ cup chopped red bell pepper
6 fat-free or nearly fat-free franks, chopped into small pieces
One 15.5-ounce can Hunt's Manwich Original Sloppy Joe Sauce
6 light hot dog buns (about 80 calories each)

o Directions

Bring a pot sprayed with nonstick spray to medium-high heat. Add onion, bell pepper, and franks, and cook for 6 to 8 minutes, until veggies are browned and franks are just slightly crispy.

Reduce heat to medium and add sauce. Stirring occasionally, cook until heated throughout.

HG Tip!

For more sloppy deliciousness, check out the nuke 'n chew Sloppy Joe-chiladas on page 84!

Evenly distribute sloppy frank mixture among the hot dog buns, about ½ cup mixture per bun. Serve and enjoy!

MAKES 6 SERVINGS

HG Alternative!

Can't find 80-calorie buns? No worries! Get the lowest-calorie ones you can find, and adjust the nutritionals for this recipe accordingly.

holy moly cannoli cones

These might actually be the cutest food items in the entire book. But let's put adorableness aside for a moment . . . they TASTE AWESOME!!! Try serving these at parties and your events will immediately become 37 percent more enjoyable.

> **PER SERVING** (1 cannoli cone): 134 calories, 1.75g fat, 184mg sodium, 21g carbs, 0g fiber, 10.5g sugars, 6g protein

o Ingredients

1 cup plus 2 tablespoons fat-free ricotta cheese

⅔ cup Cool Whip Free, thawed

2½ tablespoons Splenda No Calorie Sweetener (granulated)

1 tablespoon sugar-free fat-free vanilla instant pudding mix

1 tablespoon powdered sugar

2 tablespoons mini semi-sweet chocolate chips, divided

6 sugar cones (like the kind by Keebler)

o Directions

Place all ingredients except chocolate chips and sugar cones in a medium bowl. Using a handheld electric mixer set to high speed, mix until fully combined and fluffy. Fold in half of the chocolate chips.

Transfer mixture to a large plastic bag, squeezing it down toward one bottom corner of the bag. Snip that corner off with scissors, so that you have a makeshift piping bag.

Gently squeeze the ricotta mixture into the cones, evenly distributing it among them.

Sprinkle the remaining chocolate chips evenly on top of the filling in each cone.

Eat and enjoy!

MAKES 6 SERVINGS

For a pic of this recipe, see the second photo insert. Yay!

HG Alternative!

If you can't find fat-free ricotta, go for low-fat or light—then each Cannoli Cone would have 145 calories and 4 grams of fat.

For more recipes, tips & tricks, food finds, and MORE, sign up for FREE daily emails at hungry-girl.com!

You'll Need: bowl, rolling pin, pizza cutter (optional), 12-cup muffin pan, pastry brush (optional)
Prep: 20 minutes   **Cook:** 15 minutes

jammin' tarts

These are sooooo cute . . . and sweet . . . and fruity . . . and yummy . . . and fun. And that's all I have to say about 'em. Oh, they're also easy to make. Okay, now I'm done.

> **PER SERVING** (1 tart): 43 calories, 1.5g fat, 80mg sodium, 8.5g carbs, <0.5g fiber, 1g sugars, 1g protein

o Ingredients

½ cup sugar-free jam or preserves (any flavor)
1 teaspoon cornstarch
Dash salt
1 tablespoon flour
½ package Pillsbury Crescent Recipe Creations Seamless Dough Sheet
1 egg white or 2 tablespoons liquid egg whites
1 tablespoon powdered sugar

o Directions

Preheat oven to 350 degrees.

In a small bowl, thoroughly mix jam, cornstarch, and salt, and set aside.

Prepare a dry surface by dusting it with some of the flour. Dust a rolling pin with the flour, as well.

Roll dough out to about ⅛-inch thickness. Using a knife or pizza cutter, cut into 12 squares.

Place each square into a cup of a 12-cup muffin pan, and press it into the bottom and sides, creating a little dough "cup" about ½-inch tall.

Using a pastry brush or your fingers, lightly brush dough cups with a thin layer of egg white. (You do not need to use all the egg white.) Spoon 2 teaspoons jam mixture into the center of each cup, leaving room around the edges for it to melt and spread.

Bake in the oven for 10 to 12 minutes, until dough cups start to turn golden brown. Let cool for several minutes.

If needed, run a knife along the edges of the tarts to release them from the pan. Sprinkle with sugar and enjoy!

MAKES 12 SERVINGS

 For a pic of this recipe, see the second photo insert. Yay!

Extra, Extra!

It's best to use the refrigerated dough soon after you open it. So make a second batch of this recipe ASAP, or make some Creamed Corn–Cheese Bites (page 102)!

frosted apple pie cupcakes

These cupcakes are perfectly apple-y with a sweet cinnamon frosting.
I LOVE CUPCAKES!!!

PER SERVING (1 frosted cupcake): 155 calories, 2.5g fat, 308mg sodium, 30g carbs, 0.75g fiber, 16.5g sugars, 3g protein

o Ingredients

For Frosting
1 cup Cool Whip Free, thawed
3 tablespoons fat-free cream cheese,
    room temperature
½ tablespoon sugar-free fat-free vanilla
    instant pudding mix
¾ teaspoon cinnamon
1 no-calorie sweetener packet

For Cupcakes
2 cups moist-style yellow cake mix
2 cups peeled and finely chopped Fuji apples
½ cup no-sugar-added applesauce
½ cup fat-free liquid egg substitute
¼ cup fat-free sour cream
1 tablespoon cinnamon
1 teaspoon baking powder
⅛ teaspoon salt

o Directions

Preheat oven to 350 degrees.

Combine all of the frosting ingredients in a bowl and mix well. Refrigerate until cupcakes are ready to be frosted.

Combine all of the cupcake ingredients in a large bowl, and mix until blended.

Line a 12-cup muffin pan with baking cups and/or spray with nonstick spray. Evenly distribute cake mixture among the cups.

Bake in the oven for about 15 minutes, until a toothpick inserted into the center of a cupcake comes out clean.

Let cool completely, and then evenly distribute frosting among the tops of the cupcakes. Enjoy!

MAKES 12 SERVINGS

HG Tip!

Want more cupcake recipes? There's an entire chapter of 'em in *Hungry Girl 200 Under 200: 200 Recipes Under 200 calories*. YAY!

chapter twelve

Fun with . . .
Broccoli
Cole Slaw

Who would have thought that shredded broccoli, cabbage, and carrots could create such a stir?!

Not us. But there's little this shredded veggie trio can't do. It makes amazing slaws, salads, pasta swaps, stir-frys, and more. Broccoli Cole Slaw for president!

sweet 'n chunky turkey slaw

This is one of my go-to midday meals. I love the sweetness of the raisins and apple chunks mixed with the slaw and turkey. SOOOO GOOOOD!

PER SERVING (¼th of recipe, about 1½ cups): 236 calories, 1g fat, 325mg sodium, 28g carbs, 4.5g fiber, 16.5g sugars, 28g protein

○ Ingredients

One 12-ounce bag (4 cups) dry broccoli cole slaw
12 ounces cooked boneless skinless lean turkey breast, cubed
1 large Fuji apple, cored and diced
¼ cup raisins (not packed)
¼ cup plus two tablespoons fat-free honey mustard dressing

○ Directions

Toss all ingredients together in a large bowl. Mix well.

Cover and refrigerate for at least 2 hours, or until ready to serve. Enjoy!

MAKES 4 SERVINGS

bacon ranch broccoli slaw

Does bacon really make EVERYTHING better? Not quite sure, but it definitely works in this recipe.

> **PER SERVING** (¼th of recipe, about 1 cup): 96 calories, 2.5g fat, 635mg sodium, 11.5g carbs, 3g fiber, 6g sugars, 6.5g protein

○ Ingredients

⅔ cup fat-free sour cream
1½ tablespoons dry ranch dressing/dip seasoning mix
One 12-ounce bag (4 cups) dry broccoli cole slaw
¼ cup precooked real crumbled bacon

○ Directions

Combine sour cream and seasoning mix in a large bowl and stir thoroughly.

Add slaw and toss to coat. Add bacon and mix well.

Cover and refrigerate for at least 2 hours, or until ready to serve. Enjoy!

MAKES 4 SERVINGS

teriyaki shrimp 'n slaw stir-fry

Yay, another AMAZINGLY easy and tasty shrimp meal. This one comes complete with vegetables. YES!!!

PER SERVING (1/3rd of recipe, about 1⅓ cups): 210 calories, 2g fat, 884mg sodium, 21g carbs, 4.25g fiber, 7.5g sugars, 26.5g protein

o Ingredients

1½ tablespoons cornstarch

3 tablespoons reduced-sodium/lite soy sauce

3 tablespoons sugar-free pancake syrup

3 tablespoons canned crushed pineapple packed in juice, not drained

2 teaspoons brown sugar (not packed)

2 teaspoons seasoned rice vinegar

1 teaspoon chopped garlic

¾ teaspoon Worcestershire sauce

¾ teaspoon ground ginger

One 12-ounce bag (4 cups) dry broccoli cole slaw

12 ounces raw shrimp, peeled, tails removed, deveined

o Directions

Combine cornstarch with 1 cup cold water in a pot and stir to dissolve. Add all other ingredients except broccoli cole slaw and shrimp. Mix well.

Bring the pot to medium-high heat. Stirring occasionally, cook until it reduces and thickens to a sauce-like consistency, about 10 minutes, and then remove from heat.

Bring a wok or skillet sprayed with nonstick spray to medium heat. Add slaw and cook for 5 to 10 minutes, until almost softened to desired texture.

Add shrimp to the wok/skillet and cook until opaque, about 3 minutes.

Add sauce mixture to the wok/skillet and continue to cook and stir until evenly distributed and hot.

Remove from heat and let stand for 5 minutes. Then serve and enjoy!

MAKES 3 SERVINGS

Extra, Extra!

Leftover pineapple? Make Cake on the Beach (page 88) and Slush-Puppy Pineapple Lemonade (page 194)!

For Weight Watchers **POINTS®** values and photos of all the recipes in this book, check out hungry-girl.com/book.

bbq chicken slaw

Picnics, outdoor BBQs, parties . . . they'll all be 36 percent more delicious if this slaw is included on the menu. It's SO true.

> **PER SERVING** (¼th of recipe, 1 heaping cup): 181 calories, 1.5g fat, 675mg sodium, 24.5g carbs, 4.5g fiber, 12.5g sugars, 18g protein

o Ingredients

½ cup canned tomato sauce
¼ cup ketchup
1 tablespoon plus 1 teaspoon brown sugar (not packed)
1 tablespoon cider vinegar
½ teaspoon garlic powder
One 12-ounce bag (4 cups) dry broccoli cole slaw

One 9.75-ounce (or 10-ounce) can 98% fat-free chunk white chicken breast in water, drained and flaked
1 cup sweet corn kernels, thawed from frozen
1 cup thinly sliced red onion

o Directions

Combine tomato sauce, ketchup, brown sugar, cider vinegar, and garlic powder in a large bowl, and mix until blended. Add slaw, chicken, corn, and onion, and toss until coated.

Cover and refrigerate for at least 2 hours (if you can wait!). Then DIG IN!

MAKES 4 SERVINGS

 For a pic of this recipe, see the second photo insert. Yay!

saucy pasta swap

I love pasta. A lot. This recipe will absolutely, without a doubt, satisfy your craving for garlicky, saucy, Parmesan–topped spaghetti. You're SO welcome.

> **PER SERVING** (½ of recipe, 1 heaping cup): 138 calories, 2.5g fat, 554mg sodium, 23g carbs, 8g fiber, 9g sugars, 8g protein

o Ingredients

One 12-ounce bag (4 cups) dry broccoli cole slaw
1 cup canned crushed tomatoes
3 tablespoons reduced-fat Parmesan-style grated topping
1 teaspoon garlic powder, or more to taste
Dash onion powder, or more to taste
Dash salt, or more to taste
Dash black pepper, or more to taste

o Directions

Place slaw in a large microwave-safe bowl with 2 tablespoons water. Cover and microwave for 4 to 5 minutes.

Once cool enough to handle, add tomatoes and stir. Microwave for 1 minute.

Stir in grated topping, and add seasonings to taste. Enjoy!

MAKES 2 SERVINGS

mmmmm moo shu chicken

It's moo shu madness! This recipe is perfect for anyone who loves Chinese food and thinks they have to live without moo shu forever. You don't!!!

PER SERVING (about ⅔ cup): 76 calories, 0.5g fat, 522mg sodium, 9.5g carbs, 3g fiber, 4g sugars, 8g protein

o Ingredients

3 tablespoons reduced-sodium/lite
    soy sauce
3 tablespoons seasoned rice vinegar
1 teaspoon crushed garlic
½ teaspoon cornstarch
Dash white pepper (black is fine,
    if you don't have white)
6 ounces raw boneless skinless lean
    chicken breast, cut into thin strips

One 12-ounce bag (4 cups) dry broccoli slaw
One 8-ounce can straw mushrooms, drained
½ cup canned bamboo shoots, drained
    and cut into thin strips
1 cup bean sprouts
2 tablespoons plus 2 teaspoons hoisin sauce

o Directions

In a small bowl, combine soy sauce, rice vinegar, garlic, cornstarch, and pepper. Mix well and set aside. This is your moo shu sauce.

Bring a wok or very large skillet sprayed with nonstick spray to medium-high heat. Add chicken to the skillet and cook for about 2 minutes, until no longer pink.

Add slaw to the skillet and, stirring occasionally, cook for 3 to 4 minutes, until veggies are soft.

Add mushrooms, bamboo shoots, bean sprouts, and moo shu sauce to the skillet, and mix well. Cook for an additional 3 to 4 minutes, until entire dish is hot and chicken is cooked through. Sauce will thicken as it sits.

Transfer to a serving dish and serve drizzled with hoisin sauce. Mmmm!!!

MAKES 8 SERVINGS

HG Tip!

Try our moo shu wrapped in warm low-fat flour tortillas. SO GOOD!

For more recipes, tips & tricks, food finds, and MORE, sign up for FREE daily emails at hungry-girl.com!

You'll Need: box grater, large bowl, 12-cup muffin pan, baking cups (optional), nonstick spray
Prep: 15 minutes   **Cook:** 35 minutes

turkey & veggie meatloaf minis

These are so delicious, they've inspired me to write poetry. And for the first time ever . . . it's not a haiku poem.

Turkey meatloaf minis
You are cupcake-like in many ways—
Only bursting with veggies and lean protein goodness
Instead of sugar.
And topped with ketchup instead of frosting . . .
I love you deeply.

PER SERVING (1 mini meatloaf): 142 calories, 5.25g fat, 494mg sodium, 9g carbs, 1.5g fiber, 4g sugars, 14g protein

Ingredients

1 small onion
¼ cup plus 3 tablespoons ketchup, divided
1¼ pounds raw lean ground turkey
3 cups bagged dry broccoli cole slaw,
    roughly chopped

½ cup fat-free liquid egg substitute
½ cup quick-cooking oats
2 teaspoons garlic powder
1 teaspoon salt

Directions

Preheat oven to 350 degrees.

Using a box grater, grate onion into a large bowl. Add ¼ cup ketchup and all other ingredients. Stir until thoroughly mixed.

Line 9 cups of a 12-cup muffin pan with baking cups and/or spray with nonstick spray. Evenly distribute turkey-veggie mixture among the muffin cups, and top each with 1 teaspoon ketchup.

Bake in the oven for 30 to 35 minutes, until firm with lightly browned edges. Let stand for 5 minutes before serving. Enjoy!!!

MAKES 9 SERVINGS

📷 For a pic of this recipe, see the second photo insert. Yay!

greek chicken salad slaw

Hey, Greek salad! Don't mean to pick on you, but you're not quite as interesting as this slaw. Just sayin'. BTW, thanks to Tracey for inspiring this recipe!

> **PER SERVING** (1½ cups): 149 calories, 1.5g fat, 626mg sodium, 19.5g carbs, 4g fiber, 10.5g sugars, 15g protein

○ Ingredients

One 12-ounce bag (4 cups) dry broccoli cole slaw
6 ounces cooked boneless skinless lean chicken breast, chopped
2 cups cherry tomatoes, halved
⅔ cup fat-free raspberry vinaigrette
⅔ cup thinly sliced red onion
½ cup crumbled fat-free feta cheese

½ cup canned artichoke hearts packed in water, drained and roughly chopped
¼ cup sliced black olives
1 tablespoon jarred capers, drained
½ tablespoon lime juice
1 teaspoon dried oregano
Optional: salt and black pepper

○ Directions

In a large bowl, toss all ingredients together until mixed well.

Cover and refrigerate for at least 2 hours.

Stir well before serving. If you like, season to taste with salt and pepper. Enjoy!

MAKES 5 SERVINGS

 For a pic of this recipe, see the second photo insert. Yay!

hawaiian slaw

You'll feel like hula-ing in a sassy grass skirt when you swallow a forkful of this slaw. But calm down and stay put in your own clothes, you nut. Sheesh!

> **PER SERVING** (¼th of recipe, about 1 cup): 138 calories, 1.5g fat, 658mg sodium, 22g carbs, 3.5g fiber, 15g sugars, 9g protein

o Ingredients

One 12-ounce bag (4 cups) dry broccoli cole slaw
1 cup cubed cooked ham
1 cup canned pineapple tidbits packed in juice, drained, juice reserved
½ cup fat-free sour cream
1 tablespoon seasoned rice vinegar

1 tablespoon thick teriyaki sauce with 20 to 25 calories per tablespoon
1 teaspoon Dijonnaise
1 no-calorie sweetener packet
⅛ teaspoon salt
Optional: black pepper

o Directions

Place slaw, ham, and pineapple in a large bowl. Set aside.

In a small bowl, mix all other ingredients with 1 tablespoon of the reserved pineapple juice. Add to the large bowl and toss to coat. If you like, season to taste with pepper.

Cover and refrigerate for at least 2 hours.

Mix well before serving. Eat up!

MAKES 4 SERVINGS

chapter twelve ½

Fun with . . . French Toast

Yeah, I know you're thinking an entire chapter devoted to French toast

in a book of guilt-free recipes is ironic. Or even IMPOSSIBLE. We here at HG are part evil geniuses and part magicians. And YOU'RE lucky! (And speaking of luck, I'm totally afraid of unlucky 13, so this is officially Chapter 12½!)

french-toasted waffles

What happens when you take frozen waffles and FRENCH-TOAST 'em?! Deliciousness ensues! Taste for yourself, non-believers.

PER SERVING (entire recipe): 274 calories, 6g fat, 807mg sodium, 41.5g carbs, 3.25g fiber, 6.5g sugars, 16g protein

o Ingredients

2 Eggo Nutri-Grain Low-Fat Waffles
½ cup fat-free liquid egg substitute
¼ teaspoon cinnamon
½ teaspoon vanilla extract
2 teaspoons light whipped butter or light buttery spread
1 teaspoon powdered sugar
¼ cup sugar-free pancake syrup

o Directions

Lightly toast waffles.

Mix egg substitute, cinnamon, and vanilla extract in a bowl, and set aside.

Bring a large skillet sprayed with nonstick spray to medium-high heat. Add butter and allow to coat the bottom of the skillet. Meanwhile, coat waffles thoroughly in the egg mixture.

Cook waffles for 4 to 5 minutes per side, until golden brown. Top with powdered sugar and serve with syrup for dipping!

MAKES 1 SERVING

cinnamon french toast bowl-a-rama

This kooky bowl of French toast yumminess is so easy to whip up and can be enjoyed as a breakfast, a snack, or a dessert. Yee–haaa!

> **PER SERVING** (entire recipe): 228 calories, 3g fat, 671mg sodium, 31g carbs, 6g fiber, 6g sugars, 21.5g protein

Ingredients

2 teaspoons Coffee-mate Sugar Free French Vanilla powdered creamer
2 tablespoons fat-free cream cheese, room temperature
¾ teaspoon cinnamon

¼ teaspoon vanilla extract
2 no-calorie sweetener packets
½ cup fat-free liquid egg substitute
2 slices light white bread
¼ cup Fat Free Reddi-wip
1 tablespoon sugar-free pancake syrup

Directions

Combine powdered creamer with ¼ cup hot water in a bowl, and stir to dissolve. Add cream cheese, cinnamon, vanilla extract, and sweetener, and stir vigorously until mixture is mostly uniform and free of lumps. Add egg substitute and stir. Set aside.

Toast bread and tear into cubes. Spray a large microwave-safe mug lightly with nonstick spray. Add bread cubes and top with the vanilla-egg mixture. If needed, stir gently to ensure bread is thoroughly soaked.

Microwave for 2 to 2½ minutes, until just set. Allow to cool slightly.

Fluff mixture gently with a fork. Top with Reddi-wip and drizzle with syrup. Enjoy!

MAKES 1 SERVING

You'll Need: small microwave-safe bowl, 8-inch by 8-inch baking dish, nonstick spray, medium-large bowl, handheld electric mixer

Prep: 20 minutes   Cook: 45 minutes

the big apple
french toast casserole

No-guilt French toast for a crowd. A crowd of LUCKY people. This multi-serving treat is pretty addictive, so make it for a group or you might find yourself eating multiple servings. Consider yourself alerted . . .

> PER SERVING (¼th of recipe): 232 calories, 4.25g fat, 687mg sodium, 38.5g carbs, 5.5g fiber, 8g sugars, 16.5g protein

o Ingredients

2 tablespoons light whipped butter
    or light buttery spread
8 slices light bread, cut into cubes
1 apple (preferably Fuji), cored, peeled,
    and diced
4 ounces fat-free cream cheese,
    room temperature

1¼ cups light vanilla soymilk
1 cup fat-free liquid egg substitute
1 cup plus 2 tablespoons sugar-free
    pancake syrup, divided
¼ teaspoon cinnamon
1 no-calorie sweetener packet, or more
    to taste

o Directions

Preheat oven to 350 degrees.

In a small microwave-safe bowl, microwave butter until melted. Set aside.

Spray an 8-inch by 8-inch baking dish with nonstick spray. Place bread cubes evenly along the bottom of the dish.

Sprinkle diced apple evenly over the bread.

In a medium-large bowl, combine melted butter, cream cheese, soymilk, egg substitute, 2 tablespoons syrup, cinnamon, and sweetener. If you like your French toast pretty sweet, add an extra packet of sweetener. Using a handheld electric mixer set to medium speed, mix until lump-free and smooth. Pour mixture over the bread and apple.

Make sure bread is soaked in the liquid mixture. If needed, toss lightly to coat.

Bake in the oven for about 45 minutes, until egg mixture is pretty firm and cooked through. (Be sure not to overcook, as bread could burn.) Let cool slightly.

Cut into quarters and serve with remaining 1 cup syrup for dipping. Dig in!

MAKES 4 SERVINGS

📷 For a pic of this recipe, see the second photo insert. Yay!

super-cheesy
ham-stuffed french toast

What the heck is this? It's a crazy-amazing ham-n-cheese-stuffed pile of French-toasted love. That's what it is! Enjoy it with or without syrup. (Pssst . . . Go for the syrup. Don't be a wuss.)

PER SERVING (entire recipe): 256 calories, 7g fat, 1,264mg sodium, 24g carbs, 5.25g fiber, 5g sugars, 25g protein

○ Ingredients

⅓ cup fat-free liquid egg substitute

¼ teaspoon cinnamon

2 slices light white bread

1 wedge The Laughing Cow Light Original Swiss cheese

1 slice fat-free cheddar or American cheese

1 ounce (about 2 slices) 97 to 98% fat-free ham

2 teaspoons light whipped butter or light buttery spread

Optional: sugar-free pancake syrup, for dipping

○ Directions

Combine egg substitute and cinnamon on a small plate and set aside.

Lay bread slices on a clean dry surface and spread the top of each evenly with half of the cheese wedge. Top one slice of bread with the cheese slice and ham, and then place the other slice of bread on top with the cheese-side down.

Bring a skillet sprayed with nonstick spray to medium-high heat. Add butter and allow it to coat the bottom of the skillet. Meanwhile, evenly coat both sides of your sandwich with egg substitute. Coat the sides of the sandwich as well. (You won't need to use all of the egg mixture.)

Place sandwich in the skillet and cook for 2 to 4 minutes on each side, until golden brown. If you like, serve with syrup for dipping!

MAKES 1 SERVING

cannoli-stuffed french toast nuggets

The name says it all. These li'l bites are like fat, soft, warm, chocolatey nuggets of cannoli love. Mmmmmmm!

> **PER SERVING** (entire recipe): 228 calories, 6.5g fat, 395mg sodium, 31g carbs, 3g fiber, 10.5g sugars, 12.5g protein

Ingredients

¼ cup fat-free liquid egg substitute
¼ teaspoon cinnamon
1 teaspoon vanilla extract, divided
3 tablespoons fat-free ricotta cheese
2 teaspoons mini semi-sweet chocolate chips
1 no-calorie sweetener packet
1 light hot dog bun (about 80 calories)
2 teaspoons light whipped butter or light buttery spread
½ teaspoon powdered sugar
Optional: sugar-free pancake syrup, for dipping

Directions

Mix egg substitute, cinnamon, and ½ teaspoon vanilla extract in a small bowl. Set aside.

In a separate small bowl, combine ricotta cheese, chocolate chips, remaining ½ teaspoon vanilla extract, and sweetener, and mix well.

Split hot dog bun open lengthwise, without fully separating the two halves. Spoon ricotta mixture onto the bottom half of the bun. Gently press the top half down over the filling. Carefully slice into four "nuggets."

Bring a skillet sprayed with nonstick spray to medium-high heat. Add butter and allow to coat the bottom of the skillet. Meanwhile, coat each nugget on all sides with the egg mixture. (You won't need to use all of the egg mixture.)

Once butter has melted, place nuggets in the skillet and cook for 3 to 4 minutes, flipping nuggets until golden brown on all sides.

Plate your nuggets, sprinkle with powdered sugar and, if you like, serve with syrup for dipping!

MAKES 1 SERVING

For a pic of this recipe, see the second photo insert. Yay!

HG Alternative!

If you can't find fat-free ricotta, go for low-fat or light—then your Nuggets would have 237 calories and 8.5 grams of fat.

HG Alternative!

Can't find 80-calorie buns? No worries! Get the lowest-calorie ones you can find, and adjust the nutritionals for this recipe accordingly.

overstuffed peanut butter 'n banana french toast

This recipe was inspired by something I saw on *The Best Thing I Ever Ate*. Gotta give credit where credit is due.

> **PER SERVING** (entire recipe): 327 calories, 8.5g fat, 700mg sodium, 48.5g carbs, 7.25g fiber, 11g sugars, 18g protein

○ Ingredients

⅓ cup fat-free liquid egg substitute

1¼ teaspoons vanilla extract, divided

½ teaspoon plus 1 dash cinnamon, divided

1 no-calorie sweetener packet, divided

1 tablespoon fat-free cream cheese, room temperature

2 teaspoons reduced-fat peanut butter, room temperature

2 slices light white bread

½ small banana, sliced

2 teaspoons light whipped butter or light buttery spread

¼ cup sugar-free pancake syrup

○ Directions

Combine egg substitute, 1 teaspoon vanilla extract, ¼ teaspoon cinnamon, and half of the sweetener in a bowl, and mix well. Transfer to a small plate and set aside.

In a small bowl, combine cream cheese, peanut butter, ¼ teaspoon vanilla extract, ¼ teaspoon cinnamon, and the remaining half-packet of sweetener. Mix until smooth by stirring with the handle of a fork or spoon. (That's the easiest way to mix this!)

Gently spread cream cheese—peanut butter mixture evenly onto one slice of bread. (If needed, use your fingers to help spread.) Top with banana and a dash of cinnamon, and then finish it off with the other slice of bread. Press down lightly to seal.

Bring a skillet sprayed with nonstick spray to medium-high heat. Add butter and allow to coat the bottom of the skillet. Meanwhile, evenly coat both sides of your sandwich with the egg substitute. Coat the sides of the sandwich as well. (You won't need to use all of the egg mixture.)

Place sandwich in the skillet and cook for 2 to 4 minutes on each side, until golden brown.

Serve with syrup for dipping. Enjoy!

MAKES 1 SERVING

pumpkin cheesecake french toast bites

Ooooh . . . more French-toasted nuggets of love. These taste like pumpkin-pie cheesecake. Can you handle it?!

> **PER SERVING** (entire recipe): 182 calories, 4.5g fat, 520mg sodium, 24.5g carbs, 3.5g fiber, 5g sugars, 12.5g protein

o Ingredients

¼ cup fat-free liquid egg substitute

1 teaspoon vanilla extract, divided

½ teaspoon cinnamon, divided

1 no-calorie sweetener packet, divided

1 tablespoon canned pure pumpkin

2 tablespoons fat-free cream cheese, room temperature

¼ teaspoon pumpkin pie spice

1 light hot dog bun (about 80 calories)

2 teaspoons light whipped butter or light buttery spread

2 tablespoons Fat Free Reddi-wip

Optional: sugar-free pancake syrup, for dipping

o Directions

Combine egg substitute, ½ teaspoon vanilla extract, ¼ teaspoon cinnamon, and half of the sweetener in a small bowl. Mix well and set aside.

In a separate small bowl, combine pumpkin, cream cheese, pumpkin pie spice, remaining ¼ teaspoon vanilla extract, remaining ¼ teaspoon cinnamon, and remaining sweetener. Set aside.

290

Split hot dog bun open lengthwise, without fully separating the two halves. Spoon pumpkin–cream cheese mixture onto the bottom half of the bun. Gently press the top half down over the filling. Carefully slice into four "bites."

Bring a skillet sprayed with nonstick spray to medium-high heat. Add butter and allow to coat the bottom of the skillet. Meanwhile, coat each bite on all sides with the egg mixture. (You won't need to use all of the egg mixture.)

Once butter has melted, place bites in the skillet and cook for 3 to 4 minutes, flipping until golden brown on all sides.

Plate your bites and top with Reddi-wip. If you like, serve with syrup for dipping. Enjoy!!!

MAKES 1 SERVING

HG Alternative!

Can't find 80-calorie buns? No worries! Get the lowest-calorie ones you can find, and adjust the nutritionals for this recipe accordingly.

jammed with cheese stuffed french toast

Yes, Laughing Cow Light pretty much DOES make everything better. Even fruity French toast. We know, 'cuz we tried it with cream cheese first . . .

PER SERVING (entire recipe): 263 calories, 6g fat, 860mg sodium, 42g carbs, 5.25g fiber, 4g sugars, 19g protein

o Ingredients

½ cup fat-free liquid egg substitute

¼ teaspoon cinnamon

½ teaspoon vanilla extract

2 slices light white bread

1 wedge The Laughing Cow Light Original Swiss cheese

2 tablespoons sugar-free strawberry preserves

2 teaspoons light whipped butter or light buttery spread

¼ cup sugar-free pancake syrup

o Directions

Mix egg substitute with cinnamon and vanilla extract in a bowl. Transfer to a small plate and set aside.

Lay bread slices on a clean dry surface and spread half of the cheese wedge on each slice. Spread preserves over 1 slice of bread, and place the other slice on top with the cheese-side down. Press gently to seal.

Bring a skillet sprayed with nonstick spray to medium-high heat. Add butter and allow it to coat the bottom of the skillet. Meanwhile, evenly coat both sides of your sandwich with egg mixture. Coat the sides of the sandwich as well. (You won't need to use all of the egg mixture.)

Place sandwich in the skillet and cook for 2 to 4 minutes on each side, until golden brown. Serve with syrup for dipping and enjoy!

MAKES 1 SERVING

For more recipes, tips & tricks, food finds, and MORE, sign up for FREE daily emails at hungry-girl.com!

Bonus Section: Hot Couples!

These couples are steamy alright—and there's no chance of them breaking up. And the best part is, when you hang with them, you'll NEVER feel like a third wheel.

Starring . . . Yogurt

Fat-free yogurt RULES!

* ### Fat-Free Plain Greek Yogurt + Salsa

PER SERVING (¼th of recipe, 2 tablespoons yogurt plus 2 tablespoons salsa):
24 calories, 0g fat, 208mg sodium, 3g carbs, 0.5g fiber, 2g sugars, 2g protein

For a creamy, zesty dip for four, stir together ½ cup of each until uniform in color. Serve up with chips or veggies!

* ### Fat-Free Greek Yogurt + Freeze-Dried Fruit

PER SERVING (6 ounces yogurt plus ½ cup fruit): 140 calories, 0g fat, 92mg sodium, 18.5g carbs, 1g fiber, 16.5g sugars, 16g protein

Easiest parfait ever, people. Layer yogurt and fruit in a glass, insert spoon, and commence chewing.

Cheats: *Mix a little no-calorie sweetener into the yogurt to make it sweeter!*

* ### Fat-Free Plain Greek Yogurt + Sugar-Free Pancake Syrup

PER SERVING (6 ounces yogurt plus 3 tablespoons syrup): 110 calories, 0g fat, 146mg sodium, 14g carbs, 0g fiber, 6.5g sugars, 15g protein

You'll LOVE the combo of sweet and tangy in this duo. Just drizzle and swirl syrup into yogurt. See, opposites really do attract!

* ### Fat-Free Plain Greek Yogurt + Sugar-Free Preserves

PER SERVING (6 ounces yogurt plus 2 tablespoons preserves): 110 calories, 0g fat, 64mg sodium, 16.5g carbs, 0g fiber, 6.5g sugars, 15g protein

Personalize this creamy treat with your favorite sugar-free fruit spread. Apricot is AWESOME!

* ### Fat-Free Plain Yogurt + Boneless Skinless Lean Chicken Breast

PER SERVING (2 tablespoons yogurt plus 6 ounces chicken): 204 calories, 2g fat, 134mg sodium, 2g carbs, 0g fiber, 2g sugars, 39g protein

Marinating chicken in yogurt makes it REALLY tender! Cut raw chicken into cubes, coat with yogurt, and refrigerate for at least 1 hour. (This works great in a sealable plastic bag.) Grill it on skewers or bake it, and enjoy. YUM!

Cheats: *Add your favorite spices to the yogurt.*

* Fat-Free Yogurt + Cool Whip Free

PER SERVING (6 ounces yogurt plus ½ cup whipped topping): 160 calories, 1g fat, 125mg sodium, 31g carbs, 0g fiber, 18g sugars, 5g protein

Take your favorite sweet yogurt, fluff it up with some of the whipped stuff (thawed), and freeze. It makes an icy, creamy treat. Yay!

* Fat-Free Vanilla Yogurt + Frozen Unsweetened Mixed Berries

PER SERVING (6 ounces yogurt plus 1 cup fruit): 175 calories, <0.5g fat, 100mg sodium, 32g carbs, 5g fiber, 27.5g sugars, 7g protein

Thaw your berries briefly, and stir 'em into the yogurt. BERRY exciting!!!

* Fat-Free Yogurt + Low-Fat Honey Graham Crackers

PER SERVING (6 ounces yogurt plus ½ sheet graham crackers): 130 calories, 0.5g fat, 147mg sodium, 26g carbs, <0.5g fiber, 20g sugars, 7.5g protein

Now you can make upside-down pies in almost any flavor. Just crush your crackers and sprinkle the crumbs on top of your yogurt. Key lime yogurt is PERFECT for this one!

Starring . . . Rice Cakes

These things have WAY more crunch than calories. LOVE that! Soy crisps are great too, so feel free to use them instead of the mini rice cakes. Ready . . . set . . . CHEW!

* Mini Caramel Rice Cakes + Jet-Puffed Marshmallow Creme

PER SERVING (10 mini rice cakes plus 10 teaspoons marshmallow creme): 152 calories, 0.75g fat, 229mg sodium, 36.5g carbs, 0g fiber, 20g sugars, 1g protein

Either top your cakes with a spoonful of creme, or serve 'em sandwich-style, one on top of the other!

* Caramel Rice Cakes + Cool Whip Free

PER SERVING (2 rice cakes plus ¼ cup whipped topping): 130 calories, 0.5g fat, 70mg sodium, 28g carbs, 0g fiber, 8g sugars, 2g protein

Three words, humans. ICE. CREAM. SANDWICH. Just place your Cool Whip between the cakes and FREEZE. Or use minis and make a bunch of teeny-tiny ice cream sandwiches!

* Rice Cake + Sugar-Free Preserves

PER SERVING (1 rice cake plus 2 tablespoons preserves): 69 calories, 0.5g fat, 29mg sodium, 20g carbs, 0g fiber, 2.5g sugars, 1g protein

If your rice cake needs a makeover, smear some preserves on top. Ta-da!

* Cheese-Flavored Mini Rice Cakes + Salsa

PER SERVING (10 mini rice cakes plus ⅓ cup salsa): 101 calories, 3g fat, 765mg sodium, 17.5g carbs, 1.25g fiber, 3g sugars, 2.5g protein

Why should tortilla chips have all the fun? Salsa up your rice cakes, humans. Get dippin'!

✳ Rice Cake + The Laughing Cow Light Original Swiss Cheese

PER SERVING (1 rice cake plus 1 cheese wedge): 80 calories, 2.5g fat, 420mg sodium, 9g carbs, 0g fiber, 2g sugars, 3.5g protein

Take cheese and crackers to the next level. Spread a wedge of Laughing Cow onto a lightly salted, butter-flavored, or cheddar-flavored cake. Mmmmm . . .

Cheats: *Add lean deli meat or turkey pepperoni.*

Starring...Pudding Snacks

Small cups of sugar-free pudding are not only delicious on their own, they're also AWESOME partners for a bazillion other foods. Wanna know which ones? Keep reading.

* **Jell-O Sugar Free Vanilla Pudding Snack + Mandarin Oranges Packed in Juice**

  PER SERVING (1 pudding snack plus ¼ cup oranges): 85 calories, 1g fat, 193mg sodium, 19g carbs, <0.5g fiber, 6g sugars, 1g protein

  Lightly drain the orange segments and roughly chop. Toss 'em together with pudding in a bowl and dig in! Creamsicle pudding, anyone?

* **Jell-O Sugar Free Chocolate Pudding Snack + Reduced-Fat Peanut Butter**

  PER SERVING (1 pudding snack plus 2 teaspoons peanut butter): 124 calories, 5.5g fat, 252mg sodium, 18.5g carbs, 1.5g fiber, 1g sugars, 4.5g protein

  Soften PB in the microwave for a few seconds, and then stir it into your favorite chocolatey pudding. Somewhere, a peanut butter cup is getting jealous. This is a fact.

* **Jell-O Sugar Free Vanilla Pudding Snack + Canned Pure Pumpkin**

  PER SERVING (1 pudding snack plus ½ cup pumpkin): 100 calories, 1.5g fat, 196mg sodium, 23g carbs, 3.5g fiber, 4g sugars, 2g protein

  When Thanksgiving just feels too far away, mix up this pie-inspired pudding combo. That should hold you over.

  Cheats: *Mix in some pumpkin pie spice and/or top with Fat Free Reddi-wip and crushed low-fat graham crackers.*

* Jell-O Sugar Free Vanilla or Chocolate Pudding Snack + 100-Calorie Pack Cookies

PER SERVING (1 pudding snack plus 1 pack cookies): 160 calories, 4g fat,
330mg sodium, 31g carbs, 1g fiber, 7g sugars, 2.5g protein

*Crushed cookies in pudding is soooo good! Mix 'n match with this one. Try Vanilla + Oreo
Thin Crisps, Chocolate + Planters Peanut Butter Cookie Crisps . . . and MORE!*

Starring . . . Laughing Cow Light

These creamy light cheese wedges are one of the most important ingredients in the Hungry Girl kitchen. Find them at the market in the fridge section, by the "gourmet" cheeses, or on display in the cracker section. (They're shelf-stable.) There's a reason they're used in so many HG recipes—they make almost EVERYTHING better. Here are a few quick and easy examples of how this cheese can change your life. Cow power!

* ### The Laughing Cow Light Original Swiss Cheese + 98% Fat-Free Turkey Slices

PER SERVING (1 wedge cheese plus 2 ounces turkey): 88 calories, 2.5g fat, 824mg sodium, 2.5g carbs, 0g fiber, 1g sugars, 13g protein

A super-easy, protein-packed snack. Spread a wedge onto your turkey, roll it up, and snack away!

Cheats: Spread your cheesed-up turkey with Dijonnaise and/or top with a mini pickle before rolling it up!

* ### The Laughing Cow Light Original Swiss Cheese + Salsa

PER SERVING (¼th of recipe, ½ wedge cheese plus ¼ cup salsa): 35 calories, 1g fat, 526mg sodium, 4.5g carbs, 1g fiber, 2.5g sugars, 2g protein

For HG-style salsa con queso for four, break 2 wedges of Laughing Cow into pieces and stir into 1 cup of salsa. If you like, heat until warm. Dunk things!

* ### The Laughing Cow Light Original Swiss Cheese + Apple Slices

PER SERVING (1 wedge cheese plus 1 medium apple): 130 calories, 2.25g fat, 261mg sodium, 26g carbs, 4.25g fiber, 20g sugars, 3g protein

A baggie of apple slices + a wedge of "The Cow" = tasty snack on the go. Weeeeeee!

* ### The Laughing Cow Light Original Swiss Cheese + Boneless Skinless Lean Chicken Breast

PER SERVING (1 wedge cheese plus 6 ounces chicken): 222 calories, 4g fat, 370mg sodium, 1g carbs, 0g fiber, 1g sugars, 41.5g protein

Flip to our Stuffed Chick Cordon Bleu recipe on page 94, and make it without the ham. Follow the rest of the directions, and you'll have beautiful pork-free pinwheels of chicken!

Cheats: Season the chicken with spices and/or spread on some Dijonnaise before assembling.

* ### The Laughing Cow Light Original Swiss Cheese + Fat-Free Refried Beans

PER SERVING (1 wedge cheese plus ½ cup beans): 144 calories, 2g fat, 735mg sodium, 21g carbs, 6g fiber, 2g sugars, 9.5g protein

Fat-free refried beans are tasty . . . but they're EVEN BETTER with cheese mixed into the bean mash. Heat and eat!

Cheats: Boost the cheesiness with a little fat-free shredded cheddar and/or use baked tortilla chips for dipping.

✱ The Laughing Cow Light Original Swiss Cheese + Fat-Free Liquid Egg Substitute

PER SERVING (1 wedge cheese plus ½ cup egg substitute): 95 calories, 2g fat, 490mg sodium, 3g carbs, 0g fiber, 2g sugars, 14.5g protein

TOO easy. Spray a large microwave-safe mug with nonstick spray, and pour in the Egg Beaters. Add a cheese wedge to the mug, and microwave for about a minute. Stir your cheesy egg mixture, and return it to the microwave for another 45 to 60 seconds. (Or you can just make it in a skillet like a normal scramble. Either way, it ROCKS!)

Cheats: *Season with salt, black pepper, garlic powder, etc., and/or top with salsa.*

✱ The Laughing Cow Light Original Swiss Cheese + House Foods Tofu Shirataki

PER SERVING (1 wedge cheese plus 1 bag shirataki): 75 calories, 3g fat, 290mg sodium, 7g carbs, 4g fiber, 1g sugars, 4.5g protein

Just drain and rinse noodles, blot all excess moisture with paper towels, and place in a microwave-safe bowl along with the cheese. Microwave until hot, and mix until noodles are coated. Cheesy noodle-y fun!!!

Cheats: *Add some fat-free sour cream, reduced-fat Parmesan-style grated topping, salt, and/or black pepper for Alfredo pasta fun.*

✱ The Laughing Cow Light Original Swiss Cheese + Spinach

PER SERVING (1 wedge cheese plus ½ cup cooked spinach): 56 calories, 2g fat, 323mg sodium, 4g carbs, 2g fiber, 1g sugars, 5g protein

Anyone who likes creamed spinach, listen up. Mix some steamed or heated-from-frozen spinach with this cheese, and voilà . . . Comfort food!

Cheats: *Mix in canned sliced mushrooms and/or sprinkle with reduced-fat Parmesan-style grated topping.*

✱ The Laughing Cow Light Original Swiss Cheese + Low-Fat Turkey or Veggie Chili

PER SERVING (¼ of recipe, ½ wedge cheese plus ¼ cup chili): 65 calories, 1.5g fat, 327mg sodium, 7.5g carbs, 2g fiber, 1.5g sugars, 5.5g protein

Make a guilt-free chili con queso dip! Break up 2 wedges into 1 cup of your favorite chili, and stir well. Nuke, and you've got dip for four!

Holy Moly Cannoli Cones, p. 258

Foiled Again . . . and Again . . . and Again

Mom-Style Creamy Chicken 'n Veggies, p. 146

Glaze-of-Sunshine Apricot Chicken, p. 142

Crazy Pineapple Salmon Teriyaki, p. 154

Fajitas in a Foil Pack, p. 162

Pump-Up-the-Jam Cocktail Weenies, p. 178

Hungry Chick Chunky Soup, p. 190

Chunky Veggie Pumpkin Chili, p. 176

Things That Go Blend

Slurpable Split Shake, p. 206

Chocolate-Covered-Cherries Freeze, p. 205

Creamy Caramelized Onion Bisque, p. 202

Make-Mine-Mint Cookie-rific Freeze, p. 210

Big Black-and-White Berry Parfait, p. 222

Gimme S'more Sundae, p. 223

Scoopable Creamsicle Crush Pie, p. 236

Oatmeal Raisin Softies, p. 226

Hot Fudge 'n Brownie Blitz, p. 232

EZ & Crowd-Pleasy

Jammin' Tarts, p. 260

Exploding Chicken Taquitos, p. 246

Oven-Baked Omelette Lasagna, p. 240

Corndog Millionaire Muffins, p. 250

Fun with . . . Broccoli Cole Slaw

Turkey & Veggie Meatloaf Minis, p. 274

BBQ Chicken Slaw, p. 270

Greek Chicken Salad Slaw, p. 276

Fun with . . . French Toast

The Big Apple French Toast Casserole, p. 282

Cannoli-Stuffed French Toast Nuggets, p. 286

Starring . . . Frozen Fruit

Move over, veggies! Make some room in the freezer for bags and bags of freezy fruit. Frozen fruit is a great thing to keep around, whether you eat it straight (frozen or thawed), blend it into a smoothie, or find other fun uses for it. Reminder: When you get it from the freezer aisle of the grocery store (as opposed to freezing it yourself), make sure you get the unsweetened kind, not the stuff frozen up with sugary syrup.

* **Frozen Unsweetened Peach Slices + Diet V8 Splash**

  PER SERVING (1 cup peaches plus ¾ cup juice drink): 75 calories, 0g fat, 26mg sodium, 19.5g carbs, 2.5g fiber, 12.5g sugars, 1g protein

  A quick slushie treat. Blend it up and spoon it from the glass—it's too thick to drink from a straw!

* **Frozen Unsweetened Strawberries + Light Vanilla Soymilk**

  PER SERVING (1 cup berries plus 1 cup soymilk): 122 calories, 2g fat, 105mg sodium, 21g carbs, 4g fiber, 12g sugars, 6g protein

  No time for breakfast? WRONG! Take a few seconds, blend up this quickie smoothie, and you'll be much more pleasant to be around. NO SKIPPING B-FAST!

  Cheats: *Some no-calorie sweetener and/or calorie-free sugar-free strawberry syrup work fantastically with this duo.*

* **Frozen Bananas + Cool Whip Free**

  PER SERVING (1 small banana plus 2½ tablespoons whipped topping): 109 calories, <0.5g fat, 7mg sodium, 26.5g carbs, 2.5g fiber, 13.5g sugars, 1g protein

  Cut a banana into 10 rounds and top 5 with ½ tablespoon thawed whipped topping each. Place remaining banana slices on top of the whip, and FREEZE.

  Cheats: *A little reduced-fat peanut butter swirled with the Cool Whip Free goes a looooooong way.*

Starring . . . Frozen Broccoli & Cheese Sauce

We don't know what genius decided to start freezing broccoli mixed with cheese sauce, but we want to shake his or her hand. Happy cheesy broccoli-ing!!!

✳ **Green Giant Just for One Broccoli & Cheese Sauce + Plain Light Soymilk**

PER SERVING (1 tray broccoli & cheese sauce plus ½ cup soymilk): 75 calories, 2.5g fat, 488mg sodium, 9.5g carbs, 3g fiber, 3.5g sugars, 4.5g protein

Don't cringe, this is not a smoothie! Thaw, blend, and heat for a quick broccoli & cheese soup. You can puree all of it or leave some broccoli out and then add it in afterward for some chunkiness.

Cheats: Toss some reduced-fat Parmesan-style grated topping, salt, black pepper, and/or Laughing Cow Light cheese into the blender too.

✳ **Green Giant Just for One Broccoli & Cheese Sauce + Boneless Skinless Lean Chicken Breast**

PER SERVING (1 tray broccoli & cheese sauce plus 4 ounces chicken): 189 calories, 3g fat, 586mg sodium, 7g carbs, 3g fiber, 2g sugars, 34.5g protein

Chop up grilled chicken and toss these two together or just pour the saucy veggies over a baked chicken cutlet. The broccoli comes with plenty of extra sauce to coat your meat.

Cheats: Canned sliced mushrooms love to crash this party.

✳ **Green Giant Just for One Broccoli & Cheese Sauce + Baked Potato**

PER SERVING (1 tray broccoli & cheese sauce plus one 7.5-ounce potato): 210 calories, 1.5g fat, 443mg sodium, 44g carbs, 7.5g fiber, 3.5g sugars, 6g protein

SO filling and yummy. If you want, hollow out some of the potato to make room and save calories. Tater time!

Cheats: Top with fat-free sour cream for added enjoyment.

✳ Green Giant Just for One Broccoli & Cheese Sauce + House Foods Tofu Shirataki

PER SERVING (1 tray broccoli & cheese sauce plus 1 bag shirataki): 85 calories, 2.5g fat, 460mg sodium, 13g carbs, 7g fiber, 2g sugars, 4g protein

There's TOTALLY enough sauce to go around! Make a tray of the cheesy veggies, and dump it over your drained/rinsed/patted-dry noodles. Microwave a bit longer, and then let the chewing begin!

Cheats: *A Laughing Cow Light cheese wedge, some salt, and black pepper take this couple to the next level.*

Starring . . . Broccoli Cole Slaw

Just in case you didn't get enough of the BCS (a.k.a. Broccoli Cole Slaw) in our "Fun with . . ." chapter, here are more ideas for the colorful veggie shreds!

* **Broccoli Cole Slaw + Low-Fat Sesame Ginger Dressing**

    PER SERVING (¼ of recipe, 1 cup dry slaw plus 2 tablespoons dressing): 60 calories, 1.5g fat, 415mg sodium, 10g carbs, 3g fiber, 6g sugars, 2g protein

    Mix a 12-ounce bag of slaw and ½ cup of dressing together, and let them chill in the fridge (the longer this stuff marinates, the better it'll taste!). You'll have yummy slaw for four people with almost no effort.

    Cheats: *Add chicken, sliced almonds, mandarin oranges, and/or scallions to your slaw to jazz it up. Schmancy!*

* **Broccoli Cole Slaw + Low-Calorie Thai Peanut Dressing or Sauce**

    PER SERVING (½ of recipe, 2 cups dry slaw plus 1 ½ tablespoons dressing or sauce): 100 calories, 2.5g fat, 295mg sodium, 19g carbs, 6.5g fiber, 7g sugars, 5.5g protein

    Pierce a 12-ounce bag of broccoli slaw to vent (only if the packaging says it's okay to nuke!) or transfer the veggies to a microwave steamer, and microwave for 3 to 4 minutes. Let chill completely, and then add 3 tablespoons dressing or sauce. Peanutty slaw for two. Who needs cold sesame noodles? NOT YOU!

    Cheats: *Sprinkle sesame seeds on top. Live a little!*

* **Broccoli Cole Slaw + Low-Fat Tomato Soup or Low-Fat Marinara Sauce**

    PER SERVING (½ of recipe, 2 cups dry slaw plus ½ cup soup or sauce): 120 calories, 2g fat, 525mg sodium, 21g carbs, 7.5g fiber, 12g sugars, 5.5g protein

    Place a 12-ounce (microwave-approved and pierced to vent) bag of slaw in a large microwave-safe bowl, and cook on high for 4 to 5 minutes. Mix 1 cup sauce or soup into veggies and nuke for one additional minute. It's like spaghetti for two!

    Cheats: *Sprinkle with reduced-fat Parm-style grated topping and/or mix in some ground-beef-style soy crumbles. Yum!*

✳ Broccoli Cole Slaw + Fat-Free Broth

PER SERVING (1 cup dry slaw plus 1 cup broth): 40 calories, 0g fat, 545mg sodium, 6.5g carbs, 3g fiber, 2.5g sugars, 3.5g protein

Steam your slaw slightly in a covered bowl with 1 tablespoon water. Add broth and microwave until hot. Your soup now has veggies. YES!!!

Cheats: *Toss in some chicken, shrimp, or Tofu Shirataki noodles.*

✳ Broccoli Cole Slaw + Fat-Free Liquid Egg Substitute

PER SERVING (1 cup dry slaw plus ¾ cup egg substitute): 115 calories, 0g fat, 370mg sodium, 8g carbs, 3g fiber, 3.5g sugars, 20g protein

Ooooh . . . a no-hassle garden omelette! Just cook slaw until softened in a skillet with 2 to 3 tablespoons water. Add egg substitute and scramble until cooked. SO easy!

Cheats: *Add a wedge of Laughing Cow Light or another low-fat cheese and/or top with salsa.*

Fast Food Combos

Floats and fries and wings and MORE. So easy . . . and soooooo delicious!

✱ Float! Diet Orange Soda + Fat-Free Vanilla Ice Cream

PER SERVING (1½ cups soda plus ½ cup ice cream): 100 calories, 0g fat, 199mg sodium, 21g carbs, 0.5g fiber, 4.5g sugars, 3g protein

Forget the soda fountain classic! Make your own dreamy float at home—YUM!

✱ French Fries! LesserEvil Classic SeaSalt Krinkle Sticks + Ketchup

PER SERVING (about 1 cup Krinkle Sticks plus 2 tablespoons ketchup): 140 calories, 2.5g fat, 610mg sodium, 28g carbs, 2g fiber, 8g sugars, 2g protein

No, really. They taste like crispy French fries. Next time that craving hits, grab a bag and your bottle of Heinz Ketchup. (Impostor catsups need not apply.) Pssst . . . Visit lesserevil.com to track down your Krinkles!

✱ Quesadilla! Burrito-Size Flour Tortilla (with About 110 Calories) + Shredded Fat-Free Cheddar Cheese

PER SERVING (1 tortilla plus ¼ cup cheese): 153 calories, 2g fat, 580mg sodium, 23g carbs, 6g fiber, 1g sugars, 15g protein

Quesadillas only require a tortilla and cheese. Grab some fat-free shreds, a fibered-up tortilla, and a skillet. Heat 'n eat!

***Cheats:** Live life on the edge . . . Top with fat-free sour cream and/or salsa.*

✱ Chips & Salsa! Burrito-Size Flour Tortilla (with About 110 Calories) + Salsa

PER SERVING (1 tortilla plus ¼ cup salsa): 126 calories, 2g fat, 696mg sodium, 26g carbs, 7g fiber, 3g sugars, 7g protein

Preheat oven to 400 degrees, and cut a tortilla into triangles. Arrange on a baking sheet sprayed with nonstick spray, and give the tops of the soon-to-be-chips a light mist of spray. Bake in the oven for 5 to 7 minutes, until crispy. Serve with salsa for dunking!

***Cheats:** Sprinkle with seasonings of your choosing before baking!*

✳ Burrito! Burrito-Size Flour Tortilla (with About 110 Calories) + Fat-Free Refried Beans

PER SERVING (1 tortilla plus ½ cup beans): 217 calories, 2g fat, 814mg sodium, 42g carbs, 12g fiber, 2g sugars, 13g protein

Wrap up some warm refried beans in a tortilla. Now you have a burrito. (Hint: Microwave tortilla briefly first to keep it from cracking!)

Cheats: *Add shredded fat-free cheddar and/or top with salsa and fat-free sour cream.*

✳ Caramel Apples! Apple + Light Caramel Apple Dip

PER SERVING (1 medium apple plus 2 tablespoons dip): 180 calories, 1.75g fat, 76mg sodium, 47g carbs, 3.5g fiber, 30g sugars, 1g protein

Fast food places act like they invented apples dipped in caramel. Cut up your own fruit and dunk in light caramel dip. You rock!

✳ Buffalo Wings! Boneless Skinless Lean Chicken Breast + Frank's RedHot Original Cayenne Pepper Sauce

PER SERVING (5 ounces chicken plus 2 teaspoons sauce): 180 calories, 2g fat, 595mg sodium, 0g carbs, 0g fiber, 0g sugars, 41g protein

Frank's adds Buffalo wing flavor to anything and everything. Chop cooked chicken, toss with sauce, and chew!

Cheats: *Top with reduced-fat Parm-style grated topping and/or serve with carrots, celery sticks, and light blue cheese dressing.*

Dessert Duos

Here are the best and easiest sweet-tooth-satisfying dishes.

* **Brownies! Devil's Food Cake + Canned Pure Pumpkin**

  PER SERVING (1/12 of recipe, 1 muffin): 181 calories, 3.5g fat, 357mg sodium, 37g carbs, 2g fiber, 20g sugars, 2g protein

  Mix up an 18.25-ounce box of devil's food cake mix with a 15-ounce can of pure pumpkin. THAT'S ALL! Stir until smooth (but still thick), and evenly distribute into a 12-cup muffin pan sprayed with nonstick spray. Bake at 400 degrees for 20 minutes. Eat up!

* **Banana Split! Gerber Banana Strawberry Mini Fruits + Fat-Free Vanilla Ice Cream**

  PER SERVING (1/4 cup Mini Fruits plus 1/2 cup ice cream): 133 calories, 0g fat, 99mg sodium, 28g carbs, 0.5g fiber, 10.5g sugars, 3g protein

  Freeze-dried fruit is an unconventional but very tasty ice cream topper. Mix and match your favorites!

* **Mini Cream Pies! Athens Mini Fillo Shells + Jell-O Sugar Free Pudding Snack**

  PER SERVING (3 pudding-filled shells): 64 calories, 3.25g fat, 73mg sodium, 8.5g carbs, <0.5g fiber, 0g sugars, <0.5g protein

  Prepare a 15-count box of the fillo shells according to the box directions. Take a Pudding Snack and spoon a little pudding in each shell. Eat up. Bite-sized bliss!

  Cheats: *Squirt Fat Free Reddi-wip on top or add some chopped fruit. Or be crazy and do both!*

* **Mini Snickers Pies! Athens Mini Fillo Shells + Snickers**

  PER SERVING (2 Snickers-filled shells): 91 calories, 4.75g fat, 53mg sodium, 11g carbs, <0.5g fiber, 6g sugars, <1g protein

  Cut a 2.1-ounce candy bar in half lengthwise, and then cut each half into 5 "nuggets." Set out 10 frozen fillo shells and pop a nugget into each one. Place on a baking sheet, bake in the oven for 10 minutes at 350 degrees, and then let those babies cool. INSANELY delicious.

* **Baked Apples! Apple + Diet Black Cherry Soda**

  PER SERVING (1 medium apple plus ½ cup soda): 95 calories, <0.5g fat, 16mg sodium, 25g carbs, 4.25g fiber, 19g sugars, <0.5g protein

  Just like Mom used to make! Puncture a cored Rome apple several times with a fork, place it in a baking dish, and pour a half-cup of Diet Dr Pepper over and inside of it. Bake that beauty at 350 degrees for 45 minutes until soft.

  Cheats: *Add cinnamon and/or no-calorie sweetener before baking.*

* **Caramel Hot Chocolate! 25-Calorie Diet Hot Cocoa Mix + Light Caramel Apple Dip**

  PER SERVING (1 packet cocoa plus 1 tablespoon dip): 75 calories, 0.75g fat, 172mg sodium, 17.5g carbs, 1g fiber, 10g sugars, 2g protein

  Sometimes we sip our desserts! Stir a little caramel dip into your cocoa. Why not?

  Cheats: *Top with Fat Free Reddi-wip!*

* **Rice Krispies Treats Original Bar + Sugar-Free Preserves**

  PER SERVING (1 ready-to-eat bar with 1 tablespoon preserves): 100 calories, 2.5g fat, 105mg sodium, 22g carbs, 0g fiber, 8g sugars, 0.5g protein

  Fruit attack! These preserves go everywhere, even on Rice Krispies Treats.

* **Vitalicious Triple Chocolate Chunk VitaTop + Reduced-Fat Peanut Butter**

  PER SERVING (1 VitaTop plus 1 tablespoon peanut butter): 196 calories, 7.5g fat, 258mg sodium, 30g carbs, 6g fiber, 11.5g sugars, 7g protein

  Don't even thaw that Vita. Just spread your PB on top, and sink your teeth into a totally delicious and satisfying snack. Pssst . . . Go to vitalicious.com for the muffin-top 411.

* **Rice Krispies Treats Original Bar + Fat-Free Vanilla Ice Cream**

  PER SERVING (1 ready-to-eat bar plus 2 tablespoons ice cream): 114 calories, 2.5g fat, 122mg sodium, 22g carbs, <0.5g fiber, 8g sugars, 1g protein

  Just slice a Rice Krispies Treat in half to make two wide, thin bars. Spread your ice cream evenly on top of one half, and place the other half on top. You've got a chewy ice cream sandwich. LUCKY!!!

Protein-Packed Pairs

It's the middle of the afternoon, right between lunch and dinner, and you start dragging. Reach for a little protein, baby!

* Canned 98% Fat-Free Chunk White Chicken Breast + Salsa

PER SERVING (3 ounces chicken plus ¼ cup salsa): 108 calories, 1.5g fat, 753mg sodium, 4g carbs, 1g fiber, 2g sugars, 18.5g protein

Like taco chicken but WAY faster. Just mix it up and stick a fork in it.

Cheats: Wrap it in a tortilla or add to a green salad.

* 98% Fat-Free Turkey Slices + Mini Dill Pickles

PER SERVING (2 ounces turkey plus 2 mini pickles): 63 calories, 0.5g fat, 1,144mg sodium, 3g carbs, 0g fiber, 1g sugars, 10.5g protein

Wrap cute little pickles up in snuggly blankets of lean turkey. Then DEVOUR them!

* Frozen Ground-Beef-Style Soy Crumbles + Taco Seasoning Mix

PER SERVING (⅔ cup soy crumbles plus 1 teaspoon taco seasoning mix): 87 calories, 1.5g fat, 514mg sodium, 7.5g carbs, 3.5g fiber, <0.5g sugars, 13.5g protein

An easy mixture that tastes like it escaped from a burrito. Microwave this combo together, and give yourself a Mexican-inspired protein boost!

Cheats: Toss in beans and/or top with fat-free sour cream.

* Boneless Skinless Lean Chicken Breast + Fruity Salsa

PER SERVING (6 ounces chicken plus 3 tablespoons salsa): 246 calories, 2.25g fat, 403mg sodium, 6.5g carbs, 0.5g fiber, 5g sugars, 49g protein

Smother cooked chicken in mango or pineapple salsa. The flavor is through the roof!

* Low-Fat Turkey or Veggie Chili + Boneless Skinless Lean Chicken Breast

PER SERVING (1 cup chili plus 3 ounces chicken): 298 calories, 4g fat, 905mg sodium, 28g carbs, 9.5g fiber, 5g sugars, 41.5g protein

Either chop up cooked chicken and mix it with the chili or serve a chicken cutlet smothered in the stuff. Either way, it's delicious!

Cheats: *Add guilt-free chili toppings like fat-free cheese shreds and chopped onion. DO IT!*

* Lean Ground Turkey + Ranch Dressing/Dip Mix

PER SERVING (4 ounces turkey plus 2/3 teaspoon dry mix): 168 calories, 7.5g fat, 351mg sodium, 1g carbs, 0g fiber, 0g sugars, 22.5g protein

Mix seasoning with the raw meat, and form into a patty. Bring a skillet or grill pan sprayed with nonstick spray to medium-high heat. Cook for 5 minutes per side for a tasty ranch-infused turkey burger. Mmmmm!

Cheats: *Wrap in a big crunchy lettuce leaf.*

Breakfast Twosomes

Let's put the "fast" back in breakfast! These tasty duos are easy-peasy!

* ### Fat-Free Liquid Egg Substitute + Fat-Free or Nearly Fat-Free Franks

PER SERVING (¾ cup egg substitute plus 1 frank): 134 calories, 0.5g fat, 777mg sodium, 6.5g carbs, 0g fiber, 2.5g sugars, 23.5g protein

This protein-packed scramble has FUN written all over it. Cook up a chopped hot dog in a skillet until a little crispy, add the egg, and scramble!

Cheats: *Top with ketchup.*

* ### Fat-Free Cottage Cheese + Pineapple Packed in Juice

PER SERVING (½ cup cottage cheese plus ⅓ cup pineapple): 129 calories, <0.5g fat, 427mg sodium, 18.5g carbs, 0.5g fiber, 17g sugars, 13g protein

Kind of like a throwback "diet" diner b-fast, but we love it anyway. Use chunks, tidbits, or crushed pineapple, and mix in some juice, too!

Cheats: *Add a sprinkle of no-calorie sweetener and/or shredded coconut.*

* ### Eggo Nutri-Grain Low-Fat Waffles + Sugar-Free Preserves

PER SERVING (2 waffles plus 3 tablespoons preserves): 170 calories, 2.5g fat, 410mg sodium, 42g carbs, 3g fiber, 3g sugars, 4g protein

It doesn't get more portable than this. Pop a couple of waffles in the toaster. Return several minutes later, spread preserves on one waffle, stick it to the other waffle, and GO!

* ### Fat-Free Cottage Cheese + Sugar-Free Preserves

PER SERVING (½ cup cottage cheese plus 2 tablespoons preserves): 100 calories, 0g fat, 427mg sodium, 15.5g carbs, 0g fiber, 5g sugars, 13g protein

If you think cottage cheese is too boring by itself, swirl in your favorite sugar-free preserves. Fruity sweet stuff makes mornings better. (Everyone knows this.)

It's never easy to say goodbye, so let's
NOT say goodbye. Let's say SEE YOU SOON.
Very soon. For now, you should enjoy
the more than 500 HG recipes in our
three HG cookbooks—and all of the
recipes, reviews, and food finds in the
hungry-girl.com free daily newsletter.

Back before you know it . . . 'til then—CHEW
THE RIGHT THING!

HUNGRY3

Index

A

Aloha Under the Sea, 56

AM Apple Scramble, 12

Amazin' Asian Ahi Tuna Burgers, 46

American cheese, 70, 73, 128, 138, 284

The American Classic Pita, 92

Apple Shakers, 218

apples, 116, 266, 303, 313

    AM Apple Scramble, 12

    Apple Shakers, 218

    The Big Apple French Toast
        Casserole, 282

    caramel, 311

    Double-O-Cinnamon Apple Breakfast
        Bowl, 119

    Frosted Apple Pie Cupcakes, 262

    Lucky Four-Leaf Salad with Feta
        and Apples, 22

    Super-Simple Apple-Cinnamon Dessert
        Crepes, 220

    Three-Cheese Bacon-Apple-Bella
        Frittata, 42

Asian food. *See also* **Chinese food**

    Amazin' Asian Ahi Tuna Burgers, 46

    Crab-Happy Sunomono Salad, 110

    Crazy Pineapple Salmon Teriyaki, 154

    Sweet 'n Sassy Boneless Hot Wings, 126

    Sweet-Hot Steak Bites, 188

    Teriyaki Shrimp 'n Slaw Stir-Fry, 268

    Totally Thai Chicken Lettuce Cups, 20

B

Backyard BBQ Beef Cups, 96

bacon

    The American Classic Pita, 92

    Bacon Ranch Broccoli Slaw, 267

    Big Bowl of Breakfast, 122

    BLT Pasta Salad, 82

    Blue-Ribbon Roast Beef Sandwich, 132

    Do the Cabbage Pack!, 164

    Egg Mug Lorraine, 75

    Italian-Style Bacon Alfredo Bowl, 80

    Shrimp & Grits . . . for Hungry
        Chicks!, 44

    Three-Cheese Bacon-Apple-Bella
        Frittata, 42

    Tomato Bacon Tarts, 248

    turkey, 5, 42, 92, 132, 248

banana, 166, 206, 219, 244, 288, 305, 312

BBQ Chicken Slaw, 270

BCS. *See* **Broccoli Cole Slaw**

beans, 26, 136, 148, 176, 186, 190, 200,
    252, 303, 311

beef. *See also* soy crumbles,
    ground-beef-style

    Backyard BBQ Beef Cups, 96

    Blue-Ribbon Roast Beef Sandwich, 132

    Chop-Chop Beef Stir-Fry, 32

    franks, 178

    Outside-In Cheeseburger Patty, 15

    Queen-of-the-Castle Sliders, 134

    Sweet-Hot Steak Bites, 188

bell pepper, 18, 26, 30, 36, 38, 52, 56, 58,
    65, 84, 110, 136, 148, 150, 152, 162, 172,
    184, 186, 254, 256

berries, 108, 116, 195, 197, 206, 222, 242,
    244, 297, 305

    Gazpacho Surprise, 116

    Ginormous Sweet-Tart Fruit Salad, 108

BFFs. *See* Black Forest Fillo-Cups

The Big Apple French Toast Casserole, 282

Big Black-and-White Berry Parfait, 222

Big Bowl of Breakfast, 122

black beans, 26, 136, 148, 176, 200, 252

Black Forest Fillo-Cups (BFFs), 105

BLT Pasta Salad, 82

Blue-Ribbon Roast Beef Sandwich, 132

Boca Original Meatless Burger, 36, 73, 124, 128, 130

Bowling for Pizza, 36

bread, light, 12, 14, 74, 87, 134, 281, 282, 284, 288, 292

breadbox staples, 7

breakfast. *See also* **egg mugs; French toast**

AM Apple Scramble, 12

The American Classic Pita, 92

Big Bowl of Breakfast, 122

Cinnamon French Toast Bowl-a-rama, 281

College Breakfast Burrito, 70

couples (Breakfast Twosomes), 316

Dessert Island Parfait, 219

Double-O-Cinnamon Apple Breakfast Bowl, 119

Oven-Baked Omelette Lasagna, 240

Pizza Luau, 10

Smothered Pepperoni Pizza Breakfast Burrito, 18

Three-Cheese Bacon-Apple-Bella Frittata, 42

broccoli, 32

frozen broccoli & cheese sauce, 122, 306, 307

Broccoli Cole Slaw (BCS), 5

Bacon Ranch Broccoli Slaw, 267

BBQ Chicken Slaw, 270

couples (2 ingredients) with, 308–9

Greek Chicken Salad Slaw, 276

Hawaiian Slaw, 277

Mmmmm Moo Shu Chicken, 272

Saucy Pasta Swap, 271

Sweet 'n Chunky Turkey Slaw, 266

Teriyaki Shrimp 'n Slaw Stir-Fry, 268

Turkey & Veggie Meatloaf Minis, 274

brownies, 232, 312

Buff Chick Hot Wing Dip, 86

Buffalo Vegetable Hungry Girlfredo, 83

burgers

Amazin' Asian Ahi Tuna Burgers, 46

Boca Original Meatless Burger, 36, 73, 124, 128, 130

Chili-rific Cheeseburger, 128

Egg Mug Burger-rama, 73

Happy Camper Cheeseburger Crumble, 156

Island Insanity Burger, 130

No-Buns-About-It Animal-Style Cheeseburger, 124

Outside-In Cheeseburger Patty, 15

Queen-of-the-Castle Sliders, 134

Too-Beautiful Turkey Burger, 34

Tremendous Top-Shelf Turkey Burger, 14

Bursting Burrito Bowl, 136

C

Cake on the Beach, 88

Cannoli-Stuffed French Toast Nuggets, 286

Caramel Swirl Cream Puffs, 224

Caribbean Shrimp Packets, 150

cheese. *See also* **Laughing Cow Light Original Swiss cheese**; Parmesan-style grated topping

American, 70, 73, 128, 138

cheddar, 26, 28, 42, 44, 66, 74, 76, 78, 92, 102, 122, 124, 130, 136, 246, 252, 284, 310

Cheesy Crab 'n Chile Quesadilla, 101

cream cheese, 86, 118, 220, 252, 281, 288, 290

feta, 22, 276

frozen broccoli & cheese sauce, 306, 307

mozzarella, 60, 86, 240

ricotta, 258, 286

string cheese, 10, 18, 30, 36

Cheesy Beefy Supreme Wrap, 78

Cheesy Crab 'n Chile Quesadilla, 101

Cheesy Green Eggs 'n Hamwiches, 16

cherries, 196, 204, 205, 206

Cherry Lemonade Super-Slushie, 196

chicken, 303, 306, 311, 314

BBQ Chicken Slaw, 270

Buff Chick Hot Wing Dip, 86

Bursting Burrito Bowl, 136

Chicken D'lish Kebabs, 52

Chicken Enchilada Casserole, 66

Chicken-with-a-Kick Pack, 148

Exploding Chicken Taquitos, 246

Fajitas in a Foil Pack, 162

Fiesta Bites, 252

Glaze-of-Sunshine Apricot Chicken, 142

Good Chick Lollipops, 48

Greek Chicken Salad Slaw, 276

Honey Mustard Pretzel-Coated Chicken Fingers, 24

Hungry Chick Chunky Soup, 190

Italian-Style Bacon Alfredo Bowl, 80

Mmmmm Moo Shu Chicken, 272

Mom-Style Creamy Chicken 'n Veggies, 146

Pan-Fried Chicken Parm, 60

Pizza-fied Chicken, 30

Planet Hungrywood Sweet & Cap'n Crunchy Chicken, 54

Santa Fe Cheesy Chicken Stir-Fry, 26

Slow-Cookin' BBQ Chicken, 174

Slow-Cookin' Mexican Chicken, 182

Spring Chicken Skillet, 50

Stuffed Chick Cordon Bleu, 94

Sweet 'n Sassy Boneless Hot Wings, 126

Totally Thai Chicken Lettuce Cups, 20

chili, 304, 315

Chili Cheese Dog Nachos, 138

Chili-rific Cheeseburger, 128

Chunky Veggie Pumpkin Chili, 176

EZ as 1-2-3-Alarm Turkey Chili, 186

Chilla in Vanilla Milkshake, 204

Chinese food

Chop-Chop Beef Stir-Fry, 32

Mmmmm Moo Shu Chicken, 272

Veggie-rific Fried Rice, 62

chocolate, 166, 206, 209, 210, 224, 258, 286, 300, 301, 313. *See also* Jell-O Sugar Free Chocolate Pudding Snack

BFFs (Black Forest Fillo-Cups), 105

Big Black-and-White Berry Parfait, 222

brownies, 232, 312

Chocolate-Covered-Cherries Freeze, 205

Cup o' Chocolate-Coconut Bread Pudding, 87

Easy Oven-Baked S'mores-Stuffed Bananas, 166

Expresso Cake in a Mug, 89

Hot Fudge 'n Brownie Blitz, 232

Gimme S'more Sundae, 223

Mud Pie in the Sky, 214

That's Hazel-NUTS! Cocoa Supreme, 235

Chocolate-Covered-Cherries Freeze, 205

Chop-Chop Beef Stir-Fry, 32

Chunky Veggie Pumpkin Chili, 176

Cinnamon French Toast Bowl-a-rama, 281

Coffee-mate Sugar Free French Vanilla powdered creamer, 204, 206, 209, 210

cocoa. *See* diet hot cocoa mix

College Breakfast Burrito, 70

cookies, 226, 228

Cool 'n Creamy Fruit Soup, 197

Cool Whip Free, 209, 212, 220, 224, 225, 230, 234, 236, 258, 262, 297, 298, 305

Corndog Millionaire Muffins, 250

couples (2 ingredients)

Breakfast Twosomes, 316

couples (2 ingredients) (continued)

Dessert Duos, 312–13

Fast Food Combos, 310–11

Protein-Packed Pairs, 314–15

Starring . . . Broccoli Cole Slaw, 308–9

Starring . . . Frozen Broccoli & Cheese Sauce, 306–7

Starring . . . Frozen Fruit, 305

Starring . . . Laughing Cow Light, 302–4

Starring . . . Pudding Snacks, 300–301

Starring . . . Rice Cakes, 298–99

Starring . . . Yogurt, 296–97

Crab-Happy Sunomono Salad, 110

Crazy Pineapple Salmon Teriyaki, 154

Crazy-Delicious Seafood Corn Chowder, 172

Creamed Corn-Cheese Bites, 102

Creamy Caramelized Onion Bisque, 202

Creamy Dreamy Portabella Soup, 198

crock pot

Chunky Veggie Pumpkin Chili, 176

Crazy-Delicious Seafood Corn Chowder, 172

Dan-Good Cioppino, 180

EZ as 1-2-3-Alarm Turkey Chili, 186

Glaze-of-Glory Candied Carrots, 184

Hungry Chick Chunky Soup, 190

Pump-Up-the-Jam Cocktail Weenies, 178

Slow-Cookin' BBQ Chicken, 174

Slow-Cookin' Mexican Chicken, 182

Sweet-Hot Steak Bites, 188

Turkey Mushroom Surprise, 181

Cup o' Chocolate-Coconut Bread Pudding, 87

Cupcakes, Frosted Apple Pie, 262

D

Dan-Good Cioppino, 180

Dessert Island Parfait, 219

desserts. *See also* **berries; chocolate;** Reddi-wip, Fat Free; **shakes and slushies**

Apple Shakers, 218

banana split, 312

BFFs (Black Forest Fillo-Cups), 105

Big Black-and-White Berry Parfait, 222

brownies, 232, 312

Cake on the Beach, 88

Caramel Swirl Cream Puffs, 224

Chocolate-Covered-Cherries Freeze, 205

cookies, 226, 228

Cup o' Chocolate-Coconut Bread Pudding, 87

Dessert Duos, 312–13

Dessert Island Parfait, 219

Easy Oven-Baked S'mores-Stuffed Bananas, 166

Expresso Cake in a Mug, 89

Frosted Apple Pie Cupcakes, 262

Gimme S'more Sundae, 223

Ginormous Sweet-Tart Fruit Salad, 108

Holy Moly Cannoli Cones, 258

Hot Fudge 'n Brownie Blitz, 232

Jammin' Tarts, 260

Make-Mine-Mint Cookie-rific Ice Cream Freeze, 210

Oatmeal Raisin Softies, 226

Peanut Butter Oatmeal Softies, 228

Perfect Pumpkin Bread, 242

Quickie Caramel Custard, 104

Scoopable Creamsicle Crush Pie, 236

Super-Simple Apple-Cinnamon Dessert Crepes, 220

That's Hazel-NUTS! Cocoa Supreme, 235

Upside-Down Personal Key Lime Pie, 230

Upside-Down Pineapple Crush, 234

Devil-icious Shrimp, 65

diet hot cocoa mix, 4, 87, 205, 235, 313

Dijonnaise, 14, 28, 54, 56, 72, 75, 109, 112, 114, 277, 303

Do the Cabbage Pack!, 164

Double-O-Cinnamon Apple Breakfast Bowl, 119

E

Easy Oven-Baked S'mores-Stuffed Bananas, 166

egg mugs

Egg McMuggin', 74

Egg Mug Burger-rama, 73

Egg Mug Florentine, 72

Egg Mug Lorraine, 75

Egg Mug Mexicali, 76

egg substitute, 4, 12, 14, 16, 18, 22, 24, 42, 48, 54, 60, 62, 70, 72, 73, 74, 75, 76, 87, 89, 92, 122, 126, 226, 228, 232, 240, 242, 250, 262, 274, 280, 281, 282, 284, 286, 288, 290, 292, 304, 309, 316

Eggo Nutri-Grain Low-Fat Waffles, 280, 316

English muffins, 7, 10, 16, 28, 132

Exploding Chicken Taquitos, 246

Expresso Cake in a Mug, 89

EZ as 1-2-3-Alarm Turkey Chili, 186

F

Fajitas in a Foil Pack, 162

fast and for two (or three or four)

Aloha Under the Sea, 56

Amazin' Asian Ahi Tuna Burgers, 46

Chicken D'lish Kebabs, 52

Chicken Enchilada Casserole, 66

Devil-icious Shrimp, 65

Fiesta Noodle Casserole, 51

Girl-on-Grill Veggie Wraps, 58

Good Chick Lollipops, 48

Pan-Fried Chicken Parm, 60

Planet Hungrywood Sweet & Cap'n Crunchy Chicken, 54

Shrimp & Grits . . . for Hungry Chicks!, 44

Spring Chicken Skillet, 50

Te Quiero Tequila Shrimp, 64

Three-Cheese Bacon-Apple-Bella Frittata, 42

Veggie-rific Fried Rice, 62

fast food. *See also* **burgers**; **shakes and slushies**

Big Bowl of Breakfast, 122

Blue-Ribbon Roast Beef Sandwich, 132

Bursting Burrito Bowl, 136

Cheesy Beefy Supreme Wrap, 78

Chili Cheese Dog Nachos, 138

Chili-rific Cheeseburger, 128

couples (Fast Food Combos), 310–11

Island Insanity Burger, 130

No-Buns-About-It Animal-Style Cheeseburger, 124

Queen-of-the-Castle Sliders, 134

Sweet 'n Sassy Boneless Hot Wings, 126

fat-free liquid egg substitute, *See* **egg substitute**

feta cheese, 22, 276

Fiber One bran cereal, 54, 60

Fiesta Bites, 252

Fiesta Noodle Casserole, 51

fish. *See* **seafood**

foil-pack recipes (FPRs)

Caribbean Shrimp Packets, 150

Chicken-with-a-Kick Pack, 148

foil-pack recipes (FPRs) *(continued)*

Crazy Pineapple Salmon Teriyaki, 154

Do the Cabbage Pack!, 164

Easy Oven-Baked S'mores-Stuffed Bananas, 166

Fajitas in a Foil Pack, 162

Fruity Fish Fillet Foil Packs, 168

Glaze-of-Sunshine Apricot Chicken, 142

Happy Camper Cheeseburger Crumble, 156

HG's Oven-to-Grill Foil-Pack Conversion Chart, 169

Hustle 'n Brussels Foil-Pack Attack, 160

Mom-Style Creamy Chicken 'n Veggies, 146

The Rat(atouille) Pack, 152

So-Fancy Fish Pack, 144

Stuffed 'n Squashed Mushroom Foil Pack, 158

four ingredients or less

The American Classic Pita, 92

Backyard BBQ Beef Cups, 96

Black Forest Fillo-Cups (BFFs), 105

Cheesy Crab 'n Chile Quesadilla, 101

Creamed Corn-Cheese Bites, 102

Grillin' of the Corn, 93

Quickie Caramel Custard, 104

Shrimp Cocktail Tacos, 100

Stuffed Chick Cordon Bleu, 94

Too-EZ Mac 'n Cheese, 98

franks, 5, 138, 178, 250, 256, 316

Frank's RedHot Original Cayenne Pepper Sauce, 65, 83, 86, 254, 311

freezer staples, 6

french fries, 310

French toast

The Big Apple French Toast Casserole, 282

Cannoli-Stuffed French Toast Nuggets, 286

Cinnamon French Toast Bowl-a-rama, 281

French-Toasted Waffles, 280

Jammed with Cheese Stuffed French Toast, 292

Overstuffed Peanut Butter 'n Banana French Toast, 288

Pumpkin Cheesecake French Toast Bites, 290

Super-Cheesy Ham-Stuffed French Toast, 284

fresh produce staples, 6

fridge staples, 4–5

fried rice, 62

Frosted Apple Pie Cupcakes, 262

frozen broccoli & cheese sauce, couples (2 ingredients) with, 306–7

frozen fruit. *See also* **berries**

couples (2 ingredients) with, 305

freeze-dried, 296

fruit. *See also* **apples**

banana, 166, 206, 219, 244, 288, 305, 312

berries, 108, 116, 195, 197, 206, 222, 244, 297, 305

cherries, 105, 196, 204, 205, 206

Cool 'n Creamy Fruit Soup, 197

freeze-dried fruit, 296

Fruity Bruschetta, 244

Fruity Fish Fillet Foil Packs, 168

Ginormous Sweet-Tart Fruit Salad, 108

mandarin orange, 236, 300

mango, 168, 219, 244, 314

peach, 296, 305

pineapple, 10, 56, 88, 130, 150, 154, 168, 188, 194, 234, 268, 277, 316

watermelon, 195

Fruity Bruschetta, 244

Fruity Fish Fillet Foil Packs, 168

fuji apples. *See* **apples**

G

garlic, fresh, 14 32, 44, 50, 56, 58, 64, 65
93, 116, 144, 146, 150, 152, 158, 160,
164, 172, 176, 180, 186, 198, 202, 240,
268, 272

Gazpacho Surprise, 116

Gimme S'more Sundae, 223

Ginormous Sweet-Tart Fruit Salad, 108

Girl-on-Grill Veggie Wraps, 58

Glaze-of-Glory Candied Carrots, 184

Glaze-of-Sunshine Apricot Chicken, 142

Good Chick Lollipops, 48

Greek Chicken Salad Slaw, 276

Green Giant Just for One Broccoli &
Cheese Sauce. *See* broccoli

Grillin' of the Corn, 93

ground-beef-style soy crumbles. *See* soy
crumbles, ground-beef-style

H

Happy Camper Cheeseburger
Crumble, 156

Hawaiian food

Aloha Under the Sea, 56

Cake on the Beach, 88

Dessert Island Parfait, 219

Hawaiian Slaw, 277

Island Insanity Burger, 130

Pizza Luau, 10

Holy Moly Cannoli Cones, 258

Honey Mustard Pretzel-Coated Chicken
Fingers, 24

hot cocoa. *See* diet hot cocoa mix

hot dogs. *See* franks

Hot Fudge 'n Brownie Blitz, 232

Hungry Chick Chunky Soup, 190

Hustle 'n Brussels Foil-Pack Attack, 160

I

Island Insanity Burger, 130

Italian food. *See also* **pizza**

Buffalo Vegetable Hungry Girlfredo, 83

Cannoli-Stuffed French Toast
Nuggets, 286

Dan-Good Cioppino, 180

Devil-icious Shrimp, 65

Egg Mug Florentine, 72

Fruity Bruschetta, 244

Holy Moly Cannoli Cones, 258

Italian-Style Bacon Alfredo Bowl, 80

Oven-Baked Omelette Lasagna, 240

Pan-Fried Chicken Parm, 60

Saucy Pasta Swap, 271

Sausage, Peppers, and Onions
Italia, 38

Sausage Spaghetti Swap, 77

Three-Cheese Bacon-Apple-Bella
Frittata, 42

J

Jammed with Cheese Stuffed French
Toast, 292

Jammin' Tarts, 260

Jell-O Sugar Free Chocolate Pudding
Snack, 105, 222, 224, 300, 301, 312

Jell-O Sugar Free Vanilla Pudding Snack,
88, 222, 300, 301, 312

L

**Laughing Cow Light Original Swiss
cheese**, 15, 44, 72, 74, 75, 78, 80,
83, 94, 98, 101, 109, 112, 158, 198,
284, 299

Cheesy Green Eggs 'n Hamwiches, 16

couples (2 ingredients) with, 302–4

Jammed with Cheese Stuffed French Toast, 292

lettuce, 20, 22, 34, 82, 100, 112, 124, 130, 132, 136

liquid egg substitute. See **egg substitute**

Lucky Four-Leaf Salad with Feta and Apples, 22

M

Make-Mine-Mint Cookie-rific Ice Cream Freeze, 210

mandarin oranges, 236, 300, 308

mango, 219, 244, 314

Mexican food, 298. *See also* **tortillas**; salsa

Bursting Burrito Bowl, 136

Cheesy Crab 'n Chile Quesadilla, 101

Chicken Enchilada Casserole, 66

Chili Cheese Dog Nachos, 138

College Breakfast Burrito, 70

Egg Mug Mexicali, 76

Exploding Chicken Taquitos, 246

Fajitas in a Foil Pack, 162

Fiesta Bites, 252

Fiesta Noodle Casserole, 51

Gazpacho Surprise, 116

Peachy-Keen Black Bean Soup, 200

quesadilla, 101, 310

Santa Fe Cheesy Chicken Stir-Fry, 26

Shrimp Cocktail Tacos, 100

Sloppy Joe-chiladas, 84

Slow-Cookin' Mexican Chicken, 182

Smothered Pepperoni Pizza Breakfast Burrito, 18

Te Quiero Tequila Shrimp, 64

microwave. *See also* **egg mugs**

BLT Pasta Salad, 82

Buff Chick Hot Wing Dip, 86

Buffalo Vegetable Hungry Girlfredo, 83

Cake on the Beach, 88

Cheesy Beefy Supreme Wrap, 78

College Breakfast Burrito, 70

Cup o' Chocolate-Coconut Bread Pudding, 87

Expresso Cake in a Mug, 89

Italian-Style Bacon Alfredo Bowl, 80

Sausage Spaghetti Swap, 77

Sloppy Joe-chiladas, 84

Mmmmm Moo Shu Chicken, 272

Mom-Style Creamy Chicken 'n Veggies, 146

mozzarella cheese, 60, 86, 240

Mud Pie in the Sky, 214

mushrooms, 14, 30, 32, 36, 62, 80, 84, 146, 156, 272

Creamy Dreamy Portabella Soup, 198

portabella, 34, 42, 58, 158, 176, 198, 240

Stuffed 'n Squashed Mushroom Foil Pack, 158

Turkey Mushroom Surprise, 181

N

nachos, 138

No-Buns-About-It Animal-Style Cheeseburger, 124

noodles. *See also* Tofu Shirataki Noodles

BLT Pasta Salad, 82

Buffalo Vegetable Hungry Girlfredo, 83

Fiesta Noodle Casserole, 51

Italian-Style Bacon Alfredo Bowl, 80

Saucy Pasta Swap, 271

Sausage Spaghetti Swap, 77

Too-EZ Mac 'n Cheese, 98

O

Oatmeal Raisin Softies, 226

oats, 12, 226, 228, 274

onions, 14, 18, 26, 30, 36, 38, 50, 52, 64, 65, 75, 84, 96, 124, 128, 132, 134, 136, 150, 152, 160, 162, 164, 172, 176, 178, 181, 184, 186, 188, 190, 198, 240, 248, 254, 256, 274, 278. *See also* scallions

    Creamy Caramelized Onion Bisque, 202

    red, 10, 22, 115, 116, 132, 168, 270, 276

    sweet, 56

orange soda float, 310

Oreo Thin Crisps, 210, 214

Outside-In Cheeseburger Patty, 15

Oven-Baked Omelette Lasagna, 240

Oven-to-Grill Foil-Pack Conversion Chart, 169

Overstuffed Peanut Butter 'n Banana French Toast, 288

P

pancake syrup, 5, 268, 280, 281, 282, 284, 286, 288, 292, 296

Pan-Fried Chicken Parm, 60

pantry staples, 4

Parmesan-style grated topping, 18, 30, 36, 42, 77, 80, 83, 158, 240, 248, 271

pasta. *See* **noodles**

peaches, 305

Peachy-Keen Black Bean Soup, 200

peanut butter, 228, 288, 300, 313

Peanut Butter Oatmeal Softies, 228

peas, 32, 62, 190

Perfect Pumpkin Bread, 242

pickles, dill, 28, 124, 128, 134, 314

Pillsbury Crescent Recipe Creations Seamless Dough Sheet, 96, 102, 224, 248, 260

pineapple, 10, 56, 88, 130, 150, 154, 168, 188, 234, 268, 277, 316

    Slush-Puppy Pineapple Lemonade, 194

pizza

    Bowling for Pizza, 36

    Pizza Luau, 10

    Pizza-fied Chicken, 30

    Smothered Pepperoni Pizza Breakfast Burrito, 18

Planet Hungrywood Sweet & Cap'n Crunchy Chicken, 54

potatoes, 70, 122, 156, 160, 172, 306

preserves, sugar-free, 142, 184, 206, 260, 292, 296, 298, 313, 316

Pretty-in-Pink Slushie Drink, 195

produce staples, 6

Protein-Packed Pairs, 314–15

pudding snacks, 88, 105, 222, 224, 312
    couples (2 ingredients) with, 300–301

pumpkin, pure canned, 4, 176, 208, 212, 242, 290, 300

Pumpkin Cheesecake French Toast Bites, 290

Pumpkin Pie Smoothie, 212

Pumpkin-licious Nog, 208

Pump-Up-the-Jam Cocktail Weenies, 178

Q

Queen-of-the-Castle Sliders, 134

quesadilla, 310

Quickie Caramel Custard, 104

R

The Rat(atouille) Pack, 152

Reddi-wip, Fat Free, 105, 204, 205, 206, 210, 212, 219, 222, 223, 232, 235, 236, 281, 290

refried beans, 303, 311

refrigerator staples, 4–5

rice cakes, couples (2 ingredients) with, 298–99

Rice Krispies Treats Original Bar, 313

ricotta cheese, 258, 286

S

salads

BLT Pasta Salad, 82

Crab-Happy Sunomono Salad, 110

Ginormous Sweet-Tart Fruit Salad, 108

Greek Chicken Salad Slaw, 276

Hawaiian Slaw, 277

Lucky Four-Leaf Salad with Feta and Apples, 22

Shrimped-Up Sweet Corn 'n Tomato Salad, 115

Salmon Spread the Love, 109

salsa, 66, 76, 100, 168, 200, 246 296, 298, 303, 310, 314

sandwiches. *See also* **burgers**; **tortillas**; **wraps**

Blue-Ribbon Roast Beef Sandwich, 132

Cheesy Green Eggs 'n Hamwiches, 16

Sloppy Franks, 256

Totally Terrific Tuna Melt, 28

Santa Fe Cheesy Chicken Stir-Fry, 26

Saucy Pasta Swap, 271

Sausage, Peppers, and Onions Italia, 38

Sausage Spaghetti Swap, 77

scallions, 32, 44, 46, 62, 82. *See also* onions

scallops, 56, 180

Scoopable Creamsicle Crush Pie, 236

seafood

Aloha Under the Sea, 56

Amazin' Asian Ahi Tuna Burgers, 46

Caribbean Shrimp Packets, 150

Cheesy Crab 'n Chile Quesadilla, 101

Crab-Happy Sunomono Salad, 110

Crazy Pineapple Salmon Teriyaki, 154

Crazy-Delicious Seafood Corn Chowder, 172

Dan-Good Cioppino, 180

Devil-icious Shrimp, 65

Fruity Fish Fillet Foil Packs, 168

Salmon Spread the Love, 109

Shrimp & Grits . . . for Hungry Chicks!, 44

Shrimp Cocktail Tacos, 100

Shrimped-Up Sweet Corn 'n Tomato Salad, 115

So-Fancy Fish Pack, 144

swordfish, 56

Te Quiero Tequila Shrimp, 64

Teriyaki Shrimp 'n Slaw Stir-Fry, 268

Totally Terrific Tuna Melt, 28

Yumbo Gumbo, 254

shakes and slushies

Cherry Lemonade Super-Slushie, 196

Chilla in Vanilla Milkshake, 204

Chocolate-Covered-Cherries Freeze, 205

Make-Mine-Mint Cookie-rific Ice Cream Freeze, 210

Mud Pie in the Sky, 214

Pretty-in-Pink Slushie Drink, 195

Pumpkin Pie Smoothie, 212

Slurpable Split Shake, 206

Slush-Puppy Pineapple Lemonade, 194

Toffee Crush Coffee Shake, 209

Shirataki Noodles. *See* Tofu Shirataki Noodles

shrimp

Aloha Under the Sea, 56

Caribbean Shrimp Packets, 150

Crazy-Delicious Seafood Corn Chowder, 172

Dan-Good Cioppino, 180

Devil-icious Shrimp, 65

Shrimp & Grits . . . for Hungry
Chicks!, 44

Shrimp Cocktail Tacos, 100

Shrimped-Up Sweet Corn 'n Tomato
Salad, 115

Te Quiero Tequila Shrimp, 64

Teriyaki Shrimp 'n Slaw Stir-Fry, 268

Yumbo Gumbo, 254

single meals/meals for one

AM Apple Scramble, 12

Bowling for Pizza, 36

Cheesy Green Eggs 'n Hamwiches, 16

Chop-Chop Beef Stir-Fry, 32

Honey Mustard Pretzel-Coated
Chicken Fingers, 24

Lucky Four-Leaf Salad with Feta and
Apples, 22

Outside-In Cheeseburger Patty, 15

Pizza Luau, 10

Pizza-fied Chicken, 30

Santa Fe Cheesy Chicken Stir-Fry, 26

Sausage, Peppers, and Onions
Italia, 38

Smothered Pepperoni Pizza Breakfast
Burrito, 18

Too-Beautiful Turkey Burger, 34

Totally Terrific Tuna Melt, 28

Totally Thai Chicken Lettuce Cups, 20

Tremendous Top-Shelf Turkey
Burger, 14

slaws. *See also* **Broccoli Cole Slaw;
salads**

Slammin' Slaw, 114

Sloppy Franks, 256

Sloppy Joe-chiladas, 84

Slow-Cookin' BBQ Chicken, 174

Slow-Cookin' Mexican Chicken, 182

Slurpable Split Shake, 206

Slush-Puppy Pineapple Lemonade, 194

Smothered Pepperoni Pizza Breakfast
Burrito, 18

So-Fancy Fish Pack, 144

soups. *See also* **chili**

Cool 'n Creamy Fruit Soup, 197

Crazy-Delicious Seafood Corn
Chowder, 172

Creamy Caramelized Onion
Bisque, 202

Creamy Dreamy Portabella Soup, 198

Dan-Good Cioppino, 180

Gazpacho Surprise, 116

Hungry Chick Chunky Soup, 190

Peachy-Keen Black Bean Soup, 200

Yumbo Gumbo, 254

sour cream, 48, 51, 78, 80, 82, 89, 114,
136, 138, 146, 172, 186, 200, 246, 250,
262, 267, 277

soy crumbles, ground-beef-style, 51, 76,
78, 84, 308, 314

soy sauce, reduced-sodium lite, 32, 46,
56, 62, 110, 188, 268, 272

soymilk, 5, 12, 172, 197, 204, 206, 208,
209, 210, 212, 282, 305, 306

spinach, 22, 72, 118, 240, 304

Splenda No Calorie Sweetener
(granulated), 104, 197, 220, 226, 228,
242, 250, 258

Spring Chicken Skillet, 50

stir-fry

Chop-Chop Beef Stir-Fry, 32

Santa Fe Cheesy Chicken Stir-Fry, 26

Teriyaki Shrimp 'n Slaw Stir-Fry, 268

Stuffed Chick Cordon Bleu, 94

Stuffed 'n Squashed Mushroom Foil
Pack, 158

Super-Cheesy Ham-Stuffed French
Toast, 284

Super-Simple Apple-Cinnamon Dessert
Crepes, 220

Sweet 'n Chunky Turkey Slaw, 266

Sweet 'n Sassy Boneless Hot Wings, 126

Sweet-Hot Steak Bites, 188

swordfish, 56

T

Te Quiero Tequila Shrimp, 64

teriyaki sauce, 93, 130, 154, 268, 277

Teriyaki Shrimp 'n Slaw Stir-Fry, 268

That's Hazel-NUTS! Cocoa Supreme, 235

Three-Cheese Bacon-Apple-Bella Frittata, 42

Toffee Crush Coffee Shake, 209

Tofu Shirataki Noodles, 38, 181, 304, 307. *See also* **noodles**

    BLT Pasta Salad, 82

    Buffalo Vegetable Hungry Girlfredo, 83

    Fiesta Noodle Casserole, 51

    Italian-Style Bacon Alfredo Bowl, 80

    Sausage Spaghetti Swap, 77

Tomato Bacon Tarts, 248

tomatoes, 18, 26, 34, 36 , 112, 118, 128, 130, 132

    canned/crushed, 18, 30, 36, 38, 65, 116, 176, 182, 271

    canned/diced, 176, 186

    canned/fire-roasted, 152

canned/stewed, 190, 254

cherry, 50, 276

plum, 28, 115, 240, 252

roma, 64

sun-dried/packed in oil, 82, 112

Tomato Bacon Tarts, 248

Twice-Tomatoed Turkey Tortilla, 112

Too-Beautiful Turkey Burger, 34

Too-EZ Mac 'n Cheese, 98

tortilla chips, 138

    burrito-size flour tortilla cut into, 310

tortillas, 7, 58, 66, 70, 78, 101, 118, 246, 310

    Smothered Pepperoni Pizza Breakfast Burrito, 18

    Twice-Tomatoed Turkey Tortilla, 112

Totally Terrific Tuna Melt, 28

Totally Thai Chicken Lettuce Cups, 20

Tremendous Top-Shelf Turkey Burger, 14

tuna, 28, 46

turkey, 303, 304, 314, 315

    College Breakfast Burrito, 70

    EZ as 1-2-3-Alarm Turkey Chili, 186

    Happy Camper Cheeseburger Crumble, 156

    Sweet 'n Chunky Turkey Slaw, 266

Too-Beautiful Turkey Burger, 34

Tremendous Top-Shelf Turkey Burger, 14

Turkey & Veggie Meatloaf Minis, 274

Turkey Mushroom Surprise, 181

Twice-Tomatoed Turkey Tortilla, 112

turkey bacon, 42, 92

    Blue-Ribbon Roast Beef Sandwich, 132

    Tomato Bacon Tarts, 248

turkey chili, 138, 315

    Chili Cheese Dog Nachos, 138

    EZ as 1-2-3-Alarm Turkey Chili, 186

turkey pepperoni, 30, 299

    Bowling for Pizza, 36

    Pizza-fied Chicken, 30

    Smothered Pepperoni Pizza Breakfast Burrito, 18

Twice-Tomatoed Turkey Tortilla, 112

2-ingredient recipes. *See* **couples**

U

Upside-Down Personal Key Lime Pie, 230

Upside-Down Pineapple Crush, 234

V

vanilla ice cream, 204, 206, 209, 210, 310, 313

vanilla instant pudding mix, 224, 234, 236, 258, 262

vanilla soymilk, light, 12, 197, 204, 206, 208, 209, 210, 212, 282, 305

Veggie-Packed Wrap Attack, 118

Veggie-rific Fried Rice, 62

W

Weight Watchers **POINTS**®, where to find, 19

wraps, 7. *See also* **tortillas**

Cheesy Beefy Supreme Wrap, 78

Girl-on-Grill Veggie Wraps, 58

Y

yogurt, 5, 28, 52, 58, 72, 86, 88, 104, 197, 219, 234, 236, 244

couples (2 ingredients) with, 296–97

Dessert Island Parfait, 219

Quickie Caramel Custard, 104

Scoopable Creamsicle Crush Pie, 236

Upside-Down Pineapple Crush, 234

Yumbo Gumbo, 254

DON'T MISS THESE OTHER FABULOUS HUNGRY GIRL TITLES!

Hungry Girl:
Recipes and Survival Strategies for Guilt-Free Eating in the Real World

Hungry Girl 200 Under 200:
200 Recipes Under 200 Calories

Hungry Girl Chew the Right Thing:
Supreme Makeovers for 50 Foods You Crave

Hungry Girl:
The Official Survival Guides: Tips & Tricks for Guilt-Free Eating